CONTENTS

FIGURES

PREFACE

This second edition of *Planning for Automation: A How-To-Do-It Manual for Librarians* is written for any library planning to introduce a new or replacement automated system. This manual focuses on planning for an "integrated" system, i.e., one that computerizes a multiplicity of library functions using one common database. It touches on issues ranging from initial data collection needed for the preplanning stage to actual system implementation, with the emphasis throughout on planning.

Much has changed in library automation since the first edition of this book appeared in 1992. The nature of these changes will be discussed in the Introduction. Specifically, however, in this second edition, you will find:

- greater attention paid to that part of the planning process that involves building a consensus on the goals and objectives for automating
- a new section on the preparation of a technology strategic plan
- a section on developing system specifications that focuses on the "networked" quality of today's systems
- an expanded section on training for staff and the public
- an augmented section on standards that covers transaction formats, nonprint formats, telecommunications, and the transfer of information, as well as bibliographic and item records.

As before, some issues are covered extensively, others more briefly. For readers who may want additional information about specific topics, annotated lists of sources are included at the end of each chapter. The sources selected for these lists deal with the subject material in specific, direct, and practical ways; many of them contain references and bibliographies that also may be of interest.

The Introduction offers an analysis of how changes in technology are impacting today's library and our users' expectations. Part I, "Creating a Basic Technology Plan," describes how to develop a library profile in preparation for automation, explains how to assess and identify institutional needs and priorities, and shows how to go about writing a technology plan. A technology assessment worksheet is provided for your use.

Part II, "Selecting and Implementing Systems," begins with a System Implementation Checklist. The chapters in this part discuss automation options, developing system specifications, and the process of selecting a system—from preparing the request for proposal, or "bid," through evaluating vendor proposals to making the final decision. Postselection matters—negotiating a contract with the vendor of choice, maintaining the system, and training—are also covered here. Special attention is paid to networked system requirements and specifications.

Part III, "Planning System Databases," examines the steps involved in creating and maintaining the "heart" of any system: the library's machine-readable databases. The chapters cover retrospective conversion, maintaining the bibliographic database, weeding, bar coding, and MARC. The final chapter in this part of the book discusses standards in general and identifies specific ones that are crucial to the automation endeavor. The Conclusion offers comments on the life cycle of automated systems and on the benefits of good planning for improved library services.

To wind things up, there is an Appendix that considers the consultant relationship—finding, selecting, and working with one. One section focuses specifically on ethical issues involved when using a consultant for an automation project.

Planning for Automation is a hands-on book, one that is written to provide librarians in medium-sized and smaller libraries of all types with practical advice on planning automation projects in a sensible and systematic manner. As with anything else, what appears daunting and overwhelming at first blush becomes manageable when it is demystified. Understanding the issues and getting organized are the keys to a successful automation effort, either the first time or when replacing an existing system. *Planning for Automation* provides the concepts and the tools for such an effort.

INTRODUCTION

REDEFINING LIBRARY AUTOMATION

Until the early 1990s, "automating the library" involved generally the same features as those in place since the advent of the machine-readable cataloging record in the late 1960s:

- Libraries created integrated systems in which the traditional library functions of circulation, cataloging, the public catalog, acquisitions and serials check-in were computerized using the library's database as the foundation.
- Systems usually ran on powerful supermicro-, mini-, or even mainframe computers.
- Systems were text based, incorporating no graphics, sound, or other multimedia components.
- Systems were fundamentally local, with the emphasis on controlling and accessing resources within a discrete library or network of libraries, not on accessing remote databases or library catalogs.

A veritable sea-change has occurred in the last five years, however. Library automation has undergone a transformation that reflects changing definitions of library service in general and access to resources in particular. While "planning for automation" can still be defined as planning for integrated systems that "computerize a multiplicity of library functions using a common database"—as we defined it in the first edition of this book—rapid technological change has forced a comprehensive re-examination of what automating the library really means. Thus:

- Accessible resources are no longer defined as only those residing within the library's four walls.
- The introduction of global networking capabilities to the consumer market has made information around the world as accessible as that in the immediate surroundings—maybe more so.
- Data are no longer displayed just as plain old text but also in eye-popping graphical formats.
- Dramatic drops in hardware pricing have made affordable faster machines with huge amounts of storage.

EVOLVING EXPECTATIONS

In the closing chapter of the 1992 edition of *Planning for Automation*, the authors gazed into a crystal ball and predicted:

- vastly expanded storage of indexes, statistical databases, and document databases within the library
- full-text storage of documents, complete with full-text keyword searching and on-demand printing
- access by users to library databases from home or office, with direct downloading of information and text on demand
- the ability to access remote databases across the country and the world, and to download information and text on demand
- storage of pictorial and graphic material
- the availability of "intelligent systems" providing transparent, one-step searching and access to various in-house and remote databases.

Amazingly, these predictions have all come to fruition. The public has entered cyberspace and expects its local information provider, the library, to provide the launching pad. Accordingly, today's integrated system not only must provide modules automating the traditional library functions but also must be capable of connecting through the local system into systems of other vendors, databases—bibliographic and full content, online and CD-ROM—and the Internet. Users now expect their library systems to be able to, among other things:

- provide seamless integration between system gateways and remote and local databases through the public catalog module
- allow for access by remote users to the library's resources, either by telephone or via an Internet connection
- access resources available on the Internet using a variety of graphical and multimedia-based software interfaces.

IMPLICATIONS FOR THE LIBRARY

What does this mean for your library? It means that, regardless of size and with only limited or static funding, you must as always select and manage space, collections, systems, and other information resources to meet the needs of your users, which—along with their expectations—are now changing and expanding more quickly than ever before. The big difference now is: *the library is no longer the only information game in town.*

Libraries must, therefore, plan to use a local system as a vehicle for accessing resources beyond their doors. Stimulated by the Internet (which has created universal connectivity to information resources), by interoperability standards such as Z39.50, and by computer networking architectures (such as client/server) that turn a local system into a gateway to the world, users of a library system expect to access the resources of other systems—anywhere and anytime.

Given such increased complexities and heightened levels of expectation, libraries must learn all the more how to plan effectively for automation. A crystal ball is not necessary, however, and there is little mystery involved. It is entirely a matter of building upon what you already know about your library, using tools that are readily at hand, and, most importantly, involving *from the beginning* the people who will live with the consequences: your staff and users.

SOURCES

Anderson, Carol L., and Robert Hauptman. *Technology and Information Services: Challenges for the 1990s.* Norwood, NJ: Ablex Publishing, 1993.

"For the information services practitioner and manager, this handbook offers a wealth of concrete information needed to manage technologies and its applications. It presents a conceptual framework for implementing and managing technologies, plus a detailed discussion of technologies in relation to both the needs of information and the changes that have taken place in delivering services to users."

Cohn, John M., and Ann L. Kelsey. "Planning for Automation and the Use of New Technology in Libraries." In: Ching-chih Chen, ed., *Proceedings, NIT '96: 9th International Conference, New Information Technology for Library and Information Professionals, Educational Media Specialists and Technologists.* West Newton, MA: MicroUse Information, 1996, 65–71.

The NIT conferences aim "to give librarians and information specialists from different parts of the world the opportunity to discuss their needs, interests, problems and requirements with other knowledgeable colleagues on new information technology development." The 9th NIT Conference was held in Pretoria, South Africa, in November 1996. The authors' conference presentation and paper were based largely on the earlier edition of *Planning for Automation: A How-To-Do-It Manual for Librarians* (New York: Neal-Schuman, 1992.) It gave the authors an opportunity to develop new ideas and expand on the earlier material in preparation for this revised and expanded second edition.

Saffady, William. *Introduction to Automation for Librarians.* 3d ed. Chicago: American Library Association, 1994.

We referred to the 2d edition (1989) as "a state-of-the-art survey that will remain useful as an orientation to basics in the field." The third edition reflects "the rapid technological changes of the past few years," providing new information on, among other topics, computer workstations, local area networks, integrated systems, and library functionality.

PART I: CREATING A BASIC TECHNOLOGY PLAN

Yogi Berra is quoted as having said, "You had better watch out if you don't know where you're going, because you might just get there." The process by which we get where we want to go is called planning. Simply put, *planning is the process by which we make decisions about what to do and outline how we will do it.*

In today's library environment, planning is more critical than ever. Information technology has expanded rapidly to include a wide array of systems and services that allow a library to manage locally created information and to access information scattered across the globe. It is vital to develop a *basic technology plan* as a first step in identifying which automated systems and services will best meet user needs and fulfill the mission of the library.

Given the rapidly changing nature of library technology, a *strategic planning* approach is particularly useful in developing plans for automation and technology. Strategic planning, which has become the planning method of choice over the last decade, focuses on:

- identifying key environmental issues influencing the library—for example, initiatives within a parent organization or the availability of a new technology—and the library's strategic responses to these issues
- defining a vision of service that describes ultimate outcomes but provides for flexibility in achieving these outcomes.

In short, strategic planning is most useful in situations where you can describe what you want to accomplish but are not yet sure which specific systems or technology will best allow you to accomplish it.

Developing a basic technology plan involves five steps:

1. assessing existing technology and services
2. assessing the environment and client needs
3. establishing priorities
4. developing your mission, goals, and objectives for action
5. developing a preliminary budget proposal to implement the plan.

The first three chapters of this manual take you through each of the steps involved in developing a basic technology plan. Chapter 4 then presents a simplified, two-day process for working with a group of stakeholders to conduct a basic strategic analysis and to develop a technology-focused mission, vision, goals, and objectives.

Remember, however, that your local planning process can—and should—be tailored to accommodate your resources (that is to say, your time) and your needs. There is no "perfect" planning process—only one that works!

◀1 DESCRIBING EXISTING LIBRARY SERVICES AND TECHNOLOGY

The first step in developing a technology plan is to describe existing library services and automated systems. What services are we providing in each of the basic functional areas of library service, and how much are we providing? Which technology are we currently using, and what service functions does it provide?

LIBRARY FUNCTIONS IN AN ELECTRONIC AGE

It is important to think about what we do and what we have in the broadest possible terms. In our rapidly changing times, we must "think outside the box" of traditional functions and services and make our planning horizon as wide as possible.

A basic model of library services in an electronic environment will help organize your planning efforts at each step in the process. A model that we have found particularly useful is based loosely on work by David Penniman. Our model consists of four basic functions of libraries in an electronic age:

1. providing access to the content of local resources (e.g., books, periodicals, media, electronic resources) that are part of the library's collection
2. offering gateway access to remote resources (e.g., books, periodicals, media, electronic resources), including the ability to obtain copies in print and electronic formats
3. facilitating off-site electronic access to local and remote resources from users' homes, offices, and schools
4. providing access to human assistance in locating information.

Each of these functions is described in more detail in Figure 1–1.

Figure 1–1 Library Functions in an Electronic Age

Function	Description
Access to the content of local resources that are part of the library's collection—e.g., books, periodicals, media, electronic resources	Includes the shelving and display of hard copy and other library materials as well as accessing (via library workstations) an automated catalog containing bibliographic records, locally created electronic resources, and files created by external providers and stored locally. All files can be searched by author, title, subject, and other indexed descriptors.
Access via gateway to remote resources, e.g., books, periodicals, media, electronic resources, with the ability to obtain copies in print or electronic format.	Encompasses accessing from library workstations those resources not residing at the local library. Users can search for information by author, title, subject, and other descriptors, which lead them to bibliographic records, abstracts, the full texts of documents, and other textual, graphic, and multimedia files. Materials are obtainable through online interlibrary loan request or via electronic transmission, with provision for copyright compliance and the secure transmission of billing information.
Electronic access to local and remote resources from off-site locations such as homes, offices, and schools.	Includes direct access to local library systems via telephone dial-up or through the Internet.
Access to human assistance in locating information.	This function is provided by on-site trained librarians who serve as the human interface to all information services, either in person or remotely via electronic mail, video conferencing, or online tutorials.

COLLECTING AND ORGANIZING BASIC STATISTICAL DATA

One of the most important tools a planner needs is basic statistical information on the library and its operations. Whether you are setting priorities, preparing a preliminary cost estimate, providing information for an RFP (Request for Proposal), or calculating the storage requirements for your new system, you will find that the same basic data will be needed again and again.

The Basic Data Worksheet in Figure 1–2 provides a checklist of commonly needed data. If you do not have some of this information, you can develop reasonably good estimates by either sampling a week or month in order to develop a projected annual figure or by asking one or more staff members to estimate the number. If two or more staff members agree, the figure is usually going to be close enough for planning purposes. You can collect better data while planning is under way.

DESCRIBING EXISTING LIBRARY AUTOMATION

The next step in your planning process is to describe any existing technology being used by the library. The Basic Technology Assessment Worksheet organizes information on existing automated services, data files, software and hardware (see Figure 1–3).

Hardware comprises the physical equipment that makes up an automated system, including the processor/server; storage devices such as floppy, hard- and CD-ROM drives; telecommunications equipment such as modems and routers; and other peripherals such as printers and keyboards.

Software includes the electronic program applications that allow the hardware to perform a set of functions, such as tracking circulation or cataloging.

Data files are electronic files that contain specific information to the library, such as bibliographic records, abstracts, documents, patron files, and statistical data.

Using the framework and functions given above, list those automated systems or services that are currently used in your library. What hardware does each run on? What software is employed? What data files, local or remote, are maintained or accessed on a regular basis? What kind of information do they contain and how many records are there?

It is a challenging process to develop a comprehensive, detailed inventory of existing technology and data files, but it will ultimately be worth the effort as you plan for new systems and services. It is equally important to organize your overview of systems in relation to the information access functions. This is important

---

Figure 1–2 Basic Data Worksheet

COLLECTIONS
____ Number of nonfiction book titles
____ Number of nonfiction volumes
____ Number of fiction book titles
____ Number of fiction volumes
____ Number of adult titles
____ Number of juvenile titles
____ Number of periodical/serial titles currently received
____ Number of periodical/serial titles retained but no longer currently received
____ Number of nonprint items
____ Number of government documents
____ Number of uncataloged items (paperbacks, pamphlets, clipping files, etc.)

CIRCULATION
____ Number of books circulated annually
____ Number of nonprint items circulated annually
____ Number of uncataloged items circulated annually
____ Number of reserves processed annually
____ Number of overdue notices processed annually

PATRONS
____ Number of registered patrons

ACQUISITIONS
____ Number of new items purchased annually
____ Percentage of items purchased through primary jobber
____ Percentage of items purchased directly from publishers
____ Number of standing orders

REFERENCE SERVICES
____ Number of reference transactions
____ Number of searches performed using in-house reference databases
____ Number of searches performed using remote reference databases

DOCUMENT DELIVERY SERVICES
____ Number of periodical articles requested from remote sources
____ Number of interlibrary loans requested
____ Number of interlibrary loans provided

later in the process as you examine the possibility of consolidating single function systems—the stand alone CD-ROM reference workstation is an example—into more flexible, integrated systems.

SOURCE

Penniman, W. David. "Tomorrow's Library Today." In *Special Libraries*, 78:3 (Summer 1987), 195–205.

The author reviews the (then) environment for libraries in business as well as in the public sector and offers strategies for extending library services without creating more "bricks and mortar." He describes his concept of an "information access station" that combines "the physical, electronic, and human elements of information delivery." The library functions described in this chapter are based upon the functions Penniman envisioned for his access stations.

Figure 1–3 Basic Technology Assessment Worksheet				
Function	**What automated services* are currently provided to support this function?**	**What hardware supports this service?**	**What data files currently exist to support this service?**	**What software supports this service?**
Access to the content of local resources that are part of the library's collection, e.g., books, periodicals, media, electronic resources				
Access via gateway to remote resources, e.g., books, etc., with the ability to obtain copies in print or electronic format				
Electronic access to local and remote resources from off-site locations such as homes, offices, and schools				
Access to human assistance in locating information				

Use a separate worksheet for each service.

2 ASSESSING NEEDS AND SETTING PRIORITIES

WHO NEEDS TO BE INVOLVED IN PLANNING?

Once data collection has been completed, planning can begin in earnest. Deciding who will be involved in the planning is as important as any other part of the process.

Stakeholders—those individuals who have a particular interest in the outcome of your automation efforts—should be involved in planning as much as possible. They may be internal—for example, individuals representing the different departments of your library—or external—perhaps individuals representing your parent organization or governing body—or lay persons from your community or clientele. If you are automating in cooperation with another library or libraries, participants should reflect the nature of the project.

You also want to make sure that the individuals you involve in planning will assist you in securing a favorable outcome. Users, for example, can help insure that your plans will reflect an improvement in services; representatives of your governing body or parent organization can help secure support (and funding) for your plan.

A library will often form a planning or steering committee, made up of stakeholder representatives, that will meet regularly during the planning process. Eight to twelve persons seems to be the optimum size for such a group, although larger groups may be appropriate at certain points in the process (such as for the two-day activity described in chapter 4).

NEEDS ASSESSMENT TECHNIQUES

A needs assessment essentially gathers information on what services users would like to have available from your library that they are not currently receiving. A needs assessment can be an elaborate, expensive process, or it can be as simple as a single session devoted to identifying services that should be provided or improved.

A needs assessment usually involves one or more of the following components:

- analyzing information on existing use
- distributing written user surveys
- holding focus groups, interviews, or informal discussions with users
- analyzing services provided by comparable or competitor libraries.

Existing use patterns can help to identify areas of need. Highly used services may need to be further expanded, little used services improved. Of particular benefit are any data you may gather on an ongoing basis regarding unfilled requests or user complaints.

Written surveys are frequently conducted as part of the needs assessment process. While planning groups are frequently tempted to undertake extensive surveys, the results of these surveys can be difficult to translate into specific needs. A series of short surveys will often produce much higher response rates and can be developed at specific points in the needs assessment or planning process to shed light on particular questions or issues.

Interviews or informal discussions with users can be very useful in identifying problems in existing services and systems or in discovering what your users really need but never thought to ask for. A more formal process, however, is to organize a focus group or groups. This technique consists of getting small groups of eight to twelve users together in a conducive setting to discuss specific topics and talk about the library.

Focus groups are widely used to help generate the kind of information that is difficult to obtain using written surveys, including user perceptions and needs that users may find difficult to articulate. While the selection of focus group participants should include users, almost every library has at least some existing group that can be approached to participate in a focus group-type discussion—for example, library friends, faculty members, or a corporate management team. Discussions of this type, whether formal or informal, should also be conducted with library staff.

Although focus groups work best when an outside facilitator leads the discussion, many organizations now have access to individuals with focus group experience who may be available to work with you if you do not have funding available to hire a professional. It is also possible to conduct your own focus groups with a little assistance from resource people within your organization or faculty from a neighboring college.

Finally, another useful tool for identifying needs is to examine the programs and services of other libraries serving comparable user populations, with an emphasis on those libraries that have achieved recognition for their outstanding efforts. What services do they offer that your library does not?

A Basic Needs Assessment Worksheet, which can be used to summarize the findings of your needs assessment activities, is given in Figure 2–1. Note that this worksheet encompasses the same functions as the Basic Technology Assessment Worksheet presented in chapter 1.

A Quick Guide to Conducting Focus Groups

Step 1: *Plan your focus group.*
Prepare an interview/discussion guide that states the objectives of the focus group and asks 3 to 5 questions. The questions should begin with a warm-up query, then move to more specific questions designed to elicit more detailed answers to your basic question.

Step 2: *Recruit your participants.*
Who is most likely to speak to the outcomes specified in your objectives? Who can best answer the questions in your interview guide? These are your participants.

Step 3: *Conduct the session.*
The session is conducted by a moderator, lasts 1.5 to 2 hours, and consists of three phases:

- establishing rapport with the group, structuring the rules of group interaction, and reviewing objectives
- stimulating, intense discussion on relevant topics
- summarizing the group's responses to determine the extent of agreement.

During the session, a note taker will record responses and areas of general agreement. The session may also be taped.

Step 4: *Writing up the results.*
A written report summarizes the results of the focus group based on the objectives of the session.

Figure 2–1 Basic Needs Assessment Worksheet				
Function	How is this service* being provided currently?	What problems or limitations exist with the way this service is provided?	Ideally, how should this service be provided?	What is the priority for this service based upon stakeholder input?
Access to the content of local resources that are part of the library's collection, e.g., books, periodicals, media, electronic resources				
Access via gateway to remote resources, e.g., books, etc., with the ability to obtain copies in print or electronic format				
Electronic access to local and remote resources from offsite locations such as homes, offices, and schools				
Access to human assistance in locating information				

*Use a separate worksheet for each service.

IDENTIFYING PRIORITIES

Once you have completed your needs assessment and identified possible approaches to meeting these needs, your next step will be to determine which library functions should be automated and in what order of priority.

There are typically three factors that drive automation priorities in the typical library:

- manual processes that can be performed more efficiently using technology
- new services or service improvements that are a high priority for users
- new services or service improvements that provide significant benefit in relation to cost.

To determine if a manual process is a good candidate for automation, you must assess how efficiently it is currently being performed, which requires analyzing existing manual systems. If you have an up-to-date policies-and-procedures and/or training manual, and perhaps even workflow diagrams, you are several steps ahead of your less well-documented colleagues.

The functions most often included in automated systems are:

- cataloging
- circulation
- public catalog
- acquisitions
- serials control
- access to electronic reference or document files.

In setting priorities, the questions to ask are: Which processes are repetitive and occupy large amounts of staff time? and Which require retrieval of information from large, unwieldy files? *These are the prime candidates for automation.*

Thus, if your library circulates hundreds of thousands of items a year, it's a pretty good bet that circulation will be high on your list of functions to be automated. Conversely, if you circulate only 900 items a year but check in and route 1,000 serials, circulation may not be as important to you as serials control.

High priority user needs will most likely be automation priorities as well. If your needs assessment has been successful, you should have identified one or more user needs that you are not currently meeting. If you are lucky enough to have received such clear, articulated feedback from your users (and this does not always happen), any new services or service improvements requested should be included as priorities.

Other priorities may be based on cost/benefit analyses. Will a particular new service increase client productivity? Will it eliminate manual procedures and allow staff to focus efforts on more productive activities?

Establishing your automation priorities relative to each other is important for all sorts of reasons. If needs and priorities are clear, functions can often be automated in phases, allowing for more effective use of frequently scarce funding. Evaluations of systems will be easier and more productive if you are able to match your highest functional priorities against each system's corresponding module.

Remember, there is no perfect system. Each one has strengths and weaknesses. If you are not clear as to your needs, you will be much less likely to choose a system whose strengths match your greatest needs. The checklist that follows may be useful for helping determine your needs and priorities.

ESTABLISHING PRIORITIES: A PLANNING CHECKLIST

1. Review each of the functional areas within your library in terms of the following:
   - What are the current workflow patterns and procedures?
   - How much space and equipment are used by this function?
   - What volume of activity is there in this function?
   - How much does it currently cost to perform this function?
   - What are your current problems or needs in this area?

2. Determine the relative importance of each function within your overall plan for library services.
3. Based on the above analysis, make a preliminary determination about which functions you would like to automate.
4. Do some preliminary research into what kinds of systems are available for each of the functions you plan to automate and how much they will cost.
   - How will these systems improve internal operations and/or services to your users?

- What is your staff's ability to deal with these systems, taking into account their existing levels of expertise in automation?
- How much staff time and how much of the library's financial resources can you devote to developing, implementing, and maintaining automated operations for these functions?
- Do you think you could achieve the same improvement in workflow or service without automating?

5. Based upon all of the above, decide which function(s) you plan to automate first.

SOURCES

Bremer, Suzanne W. *Long-Range Planning: A How-To-Do-It Manual for Public Libraries.* New York: Neal Schuman, 1994.

This book covers the planning process, with sections on getting organized, planning committees, taking inventory, setting goals and targeting objectives, and writing a plan. Concrete examples, timetables, worksheets, and checklists are included.

Cortez, Edwin M., and Edward John Kazlauskas. *Managing Information Systems and Technologies: A Basic Guide for Design, Selection, Evaluation, and Use.* New York: Neal-Schuman, 1986.

Chapter 2 deals with needs assessment, covering problem definition, data collection, analysis and interpretation.

Dillman, Don A. *Mail and Telephone Surveys: The Total Design Method.* New York: Wiley, 1978.

A practical guide to the design and administration of mail and telephone surveys, which suggests many ways of improving the results of survey research. A section on the relative advantages of mail, telephone, and face-to-face interviews is particularly helpful in selecting the best approach. There are checklists at the end of each section.

Greenbaum, Thomas L. *The Handbook for Focus Group Research.* San Francisco, CA: Jossey-Bass, 1993.

Revised edition of *The Practical Handbook and Guide to Focus Group Research* (1990), this book discusses focus groups–their planning, conducting, and reporting. While the book is geared to the marketing field, it does provide an overview of the technique and many examples of its use.

Hooper, Martha C. "In Crisis or Calm, Focus Groups Hit the Mark." In *Association Management* 41 (March 1989), 117–119+.

An article-length overview of the focus group technique that outlines the basic steps in the process, discusses when focus groups are useful, and gives the pros and cons of using an outside facilitator versus doing the groups yourself.

Krueger, Richard A. *Focus Groups: A Practical Guide for Applied Research*. 2d ed. Thousand Oaks, CA: Sage, 1994.

Particular attention is paid to the analysis and reporting of focus group results. The numerous examples will be especially useful to those who are just getting started.

Osborne, Larry N., and Margaret Nakamura. *Systems Analysis for Librarians and Information Professionals*. Englewood, CO: Libraries Unlimited, 1994.

"Employing basic elements from the business world, the authors show how to effectively apply systems analysis to any library setting. The book introduces readers to the steps in the process, from identifying and defining problems and collecting and analyzing data to selecting strategies for implementing and proving the system." The volume also contains useful material on flowcharting activities as part of the systems analysis process.

Sudman, Seymour, and Norman M. Bradburn. *Asking Questions: A Practical Guide to Questionnaire Design*. San Francisco, CA: Jossey-Bass, 1986.

This book gives a detailed treatment of question design, with sections on the order and format of the questionnaire, the design of telephone and mail surveys, and a step-by-step questionnaire checklist.

3 WRITING YOUR TECHNOLOGY STRATEGIC PLAN

Now that you have identified your priority needs, your final planning step is the actual writing of your technology plan.

MISSION, GOALS, OBJECTIVES

A technology plan should include the following components:

- a statement of the library's mission
- goals and objectives for the use of technology in fulfilling this mission
- activities required to accomplish these goals and objectives and their cost.

The library's mission defines why the library exists, what it is, and what it does. Most libraries already have a mission statement, but they should revisit it in light of the impact of new and emerging information technologies. It is important that you understand the mission of your parent organization, that your plan support this mission, and that your parent organization understand and accept its mission.

In addition, your plan should conform as much as possible in format and structure to other planning documents within your organization. Basic elements found in most plans are:

- A *statement of purpose*: this phrase describes an articulated mission or overall vision that frames the goals, objectives, and actions.
- *Goals:* these are broad statements of desired or intended long-term accomplishment based upon a statement of purpose.

Some examples of goals might include:

— providing users with access to a range of electronic resources that meet recurring research needs

— utilizing technology to provide cost-effective management of library resources.

Technology-related goals include those that allow new services to be offered. These would include the ability to access information that is not currently available to users or to allow information to be located or processed in new ways. Other goals can be related to increasing the effectiveness of existing services such as manual activities like cataloging, indexing, or circulation control.

- *Objectives*: these are narrower assertions of desired or intended shorter term accomplishments designed to achieve a goal. Objectives outline how or how much of the goal will be fulfilled in as concrete and specific a way as possible. If your goal is to provide access to a wide variety of databases, you will need a series of objectives indicating exactly how many, what type, and when you propose to make them available.
- *Actions*: these are measurable activities, often in a specific time frame, undertaken to achieve an objective. For the objective just cited, your actions would detail when you will issue an RFP, select a particular index or full-text file, and make that index or file available.

A Technology Planning Worksheet (given in Figure 3–1) provides a format for developing goals, objectives, and actions for library technology in your library.

In developing your written plan, it is critical that your goals and objectives be as user-oriented as possible. What you want to do is less important than what the plan will accomplish for your users. Luckily, your needs assessment work will help you to cast your plan with the user perspective in mind.

PUTTING A PRICE TAG ON YOUR TECHNOLOGY PLAN

AUTOMATION COSTS

There are eight major cost elements involved in the installation and operation of an automated system:

Figure 3-1 Technology Planning Worksheet

Statement of Purpose:

Function	Goal*	Objective*	Action*
Access to the content of local resources that are part of the library's collection, e.g., books, periodicals, media, electronic resources			
Access via gateway to remote resources, e.g., books, etc., with the ability to obtain copies in print or electronic format			
Electronic access to local and remote resources from offsite locations such as homes, offices, and schools			
Access to human assistance in locating information			

*Use a separate worksheet for each goal, objective, and action statement, since each function is likely to generate multiple goals with multiple objectives and actions in turn.

- planning and consulting costs
- purchase of system hardware and software
- purchase of network-specific hardware, software, and cabling
- telecommunications
- conversion of manual records into machine-readable form
- access, and subscriptions where appropriate, to external databases and systems
- ongoing operating costs
- additions to the system hardware and software.

When the system is shared, it is standard practice to allocate these costs among consortium members.

Planning and consulting costs include the direct (out-of-pocket) and indirect costs associated with getting started. You may need to hire a consultant to assist with long-range and/or automation planning and to involve the staff in preparing for and participating in all aspects of the automation endeavor. The costs of this process may not be immediately apparent, but remember the old adage: time is money.

Purchase of the system includes the costs of acquiring the initial system hardware and software and of preparing a site or sites for the equipment.

- *Hardware* covers the computer itself, disk drives, workstations, printers, and other machine peripherals.
- *Software* covers the function-specific modules that you buy, such as OPAC, circulation, acquisitions, and the like.
- *Site preparation* includes identifying space for the equipment and assuring proper room ventilation and, as necessary, air conditioning.
- There are also *vendor training* costs to be considered when the system is first installed.

If a system's costs are shared by two or more users, these costs may be divided equally or assigned on a proportional basis determined by a mutually agreed-upon formula.

Purchase of network-specific hardware, software, and cabling requires the design and implementation of a local area network (LAN) architecture on which the system will run. This includes the selection of appropriate wiring, network architecture, and a network operating system compatible with the system selected. Most integrated library systems now operate on LANs that not only provide access to local collections but also are gateways to the wider world of information.

PC workstations interlinked through Ethernet-based network interface cards using 10-Base T category 5 cabling wire are replacing the dumb terminals previously used by library systems. These local networks run through network operating systems, which must be compatible with both TCP/IP (Transmission Control Protocol/Internet Protocol) and with the operating system (for example, UNIX, Windows NT, Windows 95) of the automation systems selected.

Workstations connect to a server, which then connects to a wider offsite network through high-speed, broad-band digital lines utilizing connections such as ISDN (Integrated Services Digital Network), frame relay (fast transmission of digital data in a packet-switching network) and SMDS (Switched Multimegabit Data Service) with speeds ranging from 128 kilobits per second to 45 megabits per second (T3).

Telecommunications costs are no longer dealt with only by shared systems or multibranch sites. All libraries must now factor in the costs of being a gateway to global information resources. In addition to telephone company line connections, there are the expenses associated with equipment, such as data service units and routers, to connect to the Internet and to the external databases of specific vendors. When a system is shared by multiple users at different sites, this equipment is also used to link up each site's local area network into a wide area network for access to the system's servers and workstations.

Conversion costs are those associated with the creation of machine-readable bibliographic, patron, and other records that will be used by the system. Conversion expenses include staff costs—yours or an outside contractor's—associated with inputting data, as well as the machine costs of the computer actually generating the new record.

Databases and systems external to the library are now accessible through software gateways. These databases—as easily and transparently searchable as your own local catalog records—contain not only citations but also the full text of articles and books, pictures and other images, and audio and full motion video. The cost of accessing these databases, including subscription and other fees, must now be factored into every library's automation budget.

Ongoing operating costs include maintenance fees and costs for utilities, bar code labels, miscellaneous supplies, and telecommunications. If the library hires someone to manage the system, there are salary and benefit costs as well.

In a consortium, the responsibility for these expenses is usually divided among the individual members and the consortium itself.

Traditionally, cost allocation formulas have been developed based upon activity or usage levels, represented by such factors as circulation count, number of patrons, number of functions accessed, or number of services utilized. Formulas based on these criteria can be difficult to develop and maintain because they are based on variables that are subject to frequent change. An alternative is to develop a membership assessment based upon annual target goals determined by the participants and upon a formula driven by less subjective variables. See the example on pages 42–43 for one approach.

Additions to the existing system may be required to maintain performance specifications, to accommodate new users, or to allow for additional functionality. In those cases where the addition of new users requires a system upgrade, the cost of the upgrade is often charged totally or in part to the new user(s).

DEVELOPING A PRELIMINARY BUDGET

Your technology plan should also include a proposed budget, which will be the basis for the preparation of your annual budget if you control available financial resources. If, as is more likely, needed resources are not under your control, the plan and budget will form the basis for a special request to your funding source. In the case of a public library, this will be a board of trustees and municipal or county government; in the case of a special or academic library, a department/division head, CEO or chief academic or financial officer; in the case of a school library, a principal or superintendent.

The cost option information you gather in your planning will allow you to present general budget estimates for each proposed component of your plan and to document your cost proposal in detail as it is reviewed by your funding authorities.

The identification of technological options, discussed in greater detail in chapter 5, may involve a variety of activities:

- reading journals and other reference works
- having informal discussions and/or meetings with potential providers of services and systems
- visiting other "model" libraries and talking with other librarians
- commissioning a consultant's report
- gathering information through the use of formal Requests for Information (RFI) and Requests for Quotation (RFQ).

In general, discussions with other librarians and visits to other libraries are most useful in identifying realistic options and costs for your library. If a system or service is already in use by another, comparable library, you can glean how it will work in your library and how much it will cost. Keep in mind, however, that each variation in circumstances impacts the cost; the basic statistical profile you have prepared will make it easier to identify these differences as you examine systems in other libraries.

A consultant's report can be a valuable source of information on options and their approximate costs. Consultants are frequently used at this stage and are generally worth the investment if you can afford it. If you cannot afford to employ a consultant, you can still do a good job of identifying options and costs, and the extra time you spend gathering this information will increase your knowledge and understanding of the various technologies.

Once you have identified general options, your next step is to begin gathering more specific information from potential vendors. In addition to informal discussions and visits, there are two more formal mechanisms for gathering information from vendors in a more organized fashion: Request for Information (RFI) and Request for Quotation (RFQ). The RFI and RFQ are different from the Request for Proposal (RFP) or Request for Bid (RFB) (discussed in chapter 7) in that they are short (often one page) and request very specific information on products and services. In the case of the RFI, you will be gathering information on specific functions performed by a system; for the RFQ, you will be determining information on pricing. RFIs and RFQs should be used in conjunction with, but not in place of, an RFP or RFB.

Finally, there is no guarantee that your funding source will give you the resources to implement your plan. You can be sure, however, that you are far less likely to receive new resources without a plan.

SOURCES

Bryson, John M. *Strategic Planning for Public and Nonprofit Organizations: A Guide to Strengthening and Sustaining Organizational Achievement.* Rev. ed. San Francisco: Jossey-Bass, 1995.

Bryson, John M., and Farnum K. Alston. *Creating and Implementing Your Strategic Plan: A Workbook for Public and Nonprofit Organizations.* San Francisco: Jossey-Bass, 1996.

This guide and accompanying workbook offer perhaps the most concise overviews available of strategic planning, with material on the context and process of strategic change and a ten-step process for strategic planning. Sections include agreeing on a process; clarifying organizational mandates; identifying stakeholders; developing a mission and values; assessing the environment to identify strengths, weaknesses, opportunities, and threats; identifying strategic issues; developing strategies to manage the issues; adopting the strategic plan; establishing an organizational vision for the future; developing an implementation process; and reassessing strategies. The workbook consists of worksheets for each step, which take the user through the process of developing a plan.

Imhoff, Kathleen R.T. *Making the Most of New Technology: A How-To-Do-It Manual for Librarians*. New York: Neal-Schuman, 1996.

This volume "helps librarians improve library service to users by writing a technology plan; improving the technology selection decision-making process; understanding factors that can affect technology planning; and identifying the wide range of opportunities for improving information service that new technologies can offer." The book includes an "idea analysis worksheet" for use in the planning process.

Jacob, M.E.L. *Strategic Planning: A How-To-Do-It Manual for Librarians*. New York: Neal-Schuman, 1990.

"Chapters explain the variables that contribute to successful planning, including underlying assumptions, environmental considerations, strategic focus, and both personal and institutional values and priorities." Checklists, work forms, and examples are provided throughout the volume.

"Projecting Library Automation Costs; A Forum edited by Jon Drabenstott." *Library Hi Tech* 3:3 (Issue 11, 1986), 111–119.

"Five consultants address the challenge of projecting automation costs. The various cost-components of automation are identified, as are the factors that contribute most to cost miscalculation. Rules-of-thumb for projecting costs, and the risk associated with their use, are reviewed. The importance of life-cycle planning is stressed."

Riggs, Donald E. *Strategic Planning for Library Managers*. Phoenix, AZ: Oryx, 1984. *Out of print.*

"This book offers a helping hand to managers, so that they may better understand and assess where their libraries currently are, where they are going, and what the best ways are to get them to where they want to go. It is a succinct state-of-the-art document on strategic planning, including a descriptive narration of the interrelationships of the various components of a strategic plan and a 'how to do it' prescriptive approach for effective implementation."

4 A MODEL TWO-DAY PROCESS FOR DEVELOPING A BASIC STRATEGIC PLAN

One of the most effective methods of developing a basic strategic plan is by bringing a group together and working in a structured process. This chapter proposes an intensive, straightforward approach to strategic planning that emphasizes four elements:

1. providing an opportunity for library "stakeholders" to articulate their ideas, hopes, and concerns in a structured, facilitated setting
2. identifying factors in the institution's operating environment that are likely to impact on the implementation of any automation initiative
3. identifying perceptions and needs as they relate to library service
4. validating priorities for service and shaping them into a long-range, strategic plan for service and technology.

The process is designed to accomplish the above in a relatively brief period of time, minimizing its impact on people's time and work schedules. The entire process can be completed in two days. This means that the planning group members must function in a joint, collaborative mode throughout most of the process, i.e., there should be no small group or break-out sessions. However, in the interest of ensuring responses to the unique needs of, say, different libraries or groups, it may be necessary to conduct parts of the process separately. In general, the participants should be encouraged to work quickly and efficiently in order to complete in a short time what typically is accomplished over a period of weeks.

USING A FACILITATOR TO PLAN

Try to use a neutral party—a knowledgeable outside person not directly involved with your library—to facilitate the planning process. This allows the planning participants to relate to that person unencumbered by history or reporting relationships. It also insures that no one associated with the library ends up excluded from being a participant because of having to lead the process.

The planning process proposed here emphasizes collaboration that is intended to generate ideas. Once thoughts have been freely expressed through brainstorming, they are prioritized then shaped into a strategic vision encompassing a mission, goals, objectives, and actions. The process itself is the vehicle by which the final plan is created, which guarantees that the plan's conception, language, and spirit are those of the planning participants. In its final form, the plan will be a consensus document, forged through an interactive give-and-take.

STEP ONE: IDENTIFY THE PLANNING PARTICIPANTS

There are no hard-and-fast rules here except to make sure that you include representation from all those who have a stake in the outcome of your automation efforts. Invite individuals from the different departments of your library as well as lay persons from your community or clientele. If you are automating in cooperation with another library or libraries, the planning process should be collaborative from the start, and the group of participants should reflect the nature of the project.

The total number of participants should not exceed twenty-five. If you have much beyond that number, the process will become unwieldy and is likely to bog down. Do not exclude important constituencies, but keep the size of the planning group manageable.

STEP TWO: BRAINSTORMING EXERCISES

Following introductions and the obligatory logistical announcements, the planning facilitator should begin with some handouts that make important points but that do so in an easygoing, non-threatening fashion (see Figures 4–1 and 4–2). Then . . . begin to brainstorm.

EXERCISE 1

In round-robin fashion, the facilitator will ask meeting participants to identify what are referred to in strategic planning parlance as "SWOTs". These are Strengths, Weaknesses, Opportunities, and Threats that exist in the library's operating environment and are likely to impact on the outcome of any planning effort. Examples, some of which may fit more than one category, include:

"A hard-working staff that is unafraid of change."
"A staff that is averse to technology."
"A declining municipal budget."
"A clientele that is technologically literate" (or the converse).
"A board/council/CEO committed to strengthening library services."
"A rapidly-changing user population."
"A weakening local economy."

EXERCISE 2

Later, in similar round-robin style, the facilitator should engage the participants in a second brainstorming exercise to elicit their visions, perceptions, and needs pertaining to library services and technology. This can be done by posing the following question:

"What do you think should be the priorities for service in (*name of library, consortium, media center*) at the start of the twenty-first century?"

These ideas are likely to range from the very narrowly focused—"Get our patrons to return their materials on time"—to the more lofty issues—"Give our users access to resources around the world."

In both brainstorming exercises, the participants' ideas are listed on a chart as they are mentioned.

Figure 4–1   Technology Planning Project Handout: Rules of the Road

TECHNOLOGY PLANNING PROJECT
Rules of the Road

BRAINSTORMING EXERCISES

Say what you think. No idea is out of bounds . . . except:

Do not pooh-pooh other people's ideas (unless they're *really* dumb — just kidding!)

Focus on issues, not personalities.

Say what you need to say, even if it appears to repeat what someone else has said.

Be succinct.

Requests for clarification are okay; extended commentary or debate are not.

These exercises are meant to raise ideas, not build consensus. Consensus building comes later (hopefully).

Unless you are a certified Possessor of Absolute Truth, give others a chance to be heard.

Refrain from starting side conversations.

Hold routine gripes, complaints, etc., about the district for another time.

Figure 4–2 Technology Planning Project Handout: Forty Phrases That Kill Creativity

Technology Planning Project
Forty Phrases That Kill Creativity*

1. We tried that before.
2. _____ is different.
3. It costs too much.
4. That's not our job.
5. We're too busy to do that.
6. We don't have the time.
7. We don't have enough help.
8. It's too radical a change.
9. The board will never buy it.
10. It's against policy.
11. We don't have the authority.
12. Let's get back to reality.
13. That's not our problem.
14. I don't like the idea.
15. You're right, but . . .
16. You're two years ahead of your time.
17. We're not ready for that.
18. It isn't in the budget.
19. Can't teach an old dog new tricks.
20. Good thought, but impractical.
21. Let's give it more thought.
22. We'll be the laughing-stock of the library community.
23. Not that again.
24. Where'd you dig that one up?
25. We did all right without it.
26. It's never been tried before.
27. Let's put that one on the back burner for now.
28. Let's form a committee.
29. I don't see the connection.
30. It's impossible / It won't work.
31. Management will never go for it.
32. Let's all sleep on it.
33. But we've always done it this way.
34. Don't rock the boat.
35. We can't expect that from library staff.
36. Has anyone else ever tried it?
37. Let's look into it further (later).
38. Quit dreaming.
39. That's too much ivory tower.
40. It's too much work.

*Source: Edited version of FIFTY.TXT in Library 2, "Resource Co-op," of the Public Relations and Marketing Forum, CompuServe.

STEP THREE: ASSIGNING POINT VALUES

Participants should then be asked to prioritize both the environmental issues and their "visions" by assigning point values to the ideas that have been articulated by the entire group. Separately prioritize SWOT factors (as a whole and across all four factors) and visioning ideas.

The sidebar offers a simple method of assigning priority point values, one of which has the added benefit of getting everyone to move around!

A METHOD FOR ASSIGNING POINT VALUES

1. Each participant "receives" the same number of points as there are items—e.g., 50 points for 50 items—and a pack of post-its.
2. Instruct participants to distribute points as they wish, with their higher priorities getting the greater number of points.
3. Ask participants to assign no more than 10 points to any one item.
4. Instruct participants to write the number of points they are assigning in the center of the post-it, and the number of the item in the corner (that's in case the post-it falls off).
5. When everyone has finished attaching the post-it scores to the respective items, total and write in the number of points received by each item. Use a different color marker for the totals than was used to record the ideas.
6. Create a new chart listing the highest priority items.

STEP FOUR: CREATING ISSUES, GOALS, AND OBJECTIVES

Now, shape the SWOT priorities into environmental "issue areas" and the service visions into a statement of purpose, goals, objectives, and actions (refer back to chapter 3 for definitions of these terms). Together, these will constitute the long-range, strategic plan that will help to guide the library's automation efforts.

The environmental issues can either simply be included for "awareness" purposes as part of the document or be a springboard for participants to develop "strategic responses" to them. These are action steps to be taken *in response* to the perceived environmental impact. For example, a perception of "declining resources for library services" might generate a response to "organize a campaign to strengthen governmental/corporate awareness of the value of information." (*Note*: Creating strategic responses to environmental issues will likely stretch this process beyond two days.)

The mission statement/goals/objectives/actions will become the heart of the plan, establishing the basis for future technological and also other development. (Here is where you will use the Technology Planning Worksheet offered in chapter 3). Given the rapid rate of change, it is probably wise to create a plan that projects no more than three years into the future.

CONCLUSION

It must be emphasized that this is a modified strategic planning process. Its primary purpose is to give people an opportunity to express their concerns and ideas and to work with others to fashion a consensus around some basic principles. Building a fully developed strategic plan is secondary to the interaction and communication that takes place during this process. In other words, what the participants go through is at least as important as the outcome.

Finally, some benefits characterizing the process as a whole include the following:

1. People who have little or no experience with group processes will become familiar with a form of working together that is becoming more commonplace in this age of "teams" and distributed responsibility.
2. Persons who previously had little contact with one another will have an opportunity to develop a greater understanding for concerns within other areas and departments of the organization.
3. Participants are encouraged to think and then to express whatever is on their minds in a process relatively free of bureaucratic constraints.
4. Ideas become separated from the persons who expressed them, inhibiting the tendency to associate suggestions, particularly those we do not like, with the person(s) who articulated them.

PART II: SELECTING AND IMPLEMENTING SYSTEMS

The System Implementation Checklist that follows outlines a basic seven-phased process for introducing automation that is applicable to all libraries. The steps in it are covered in detail in the subsequent chapters of this part of the book.

It is important to understand that the phases outlined, although sequential in some respects, usually overlap and often take place concurrently. For example, preparing your database for conversion should begin while you are still exploring options for acquiring a system. (Note that this is true even though database conversion follows system selection and implementation in this book.) Weeding the collection, a process that is independent of automation per se, can have a major impact on the cost of any automation project and can and should be implemented immediately.

A SYSTEM IMPLEMENTATION CHECKLIST

PHASE 1: AUTOMATION OPTIONS/ALTERNATIVES

Goal: To explore courses of action that the library might take to improve services through automation.

Tasks:

1. Examine and outline alternative approaches and possibilities.
2. Define a series of steps for a phased and coordinated plan for automating the library.
3. Identify and evaluate software, hardware, and telecommunications configurations.
4. Outline start-up and ongoing costs of the proposed alternatives.
5. Determine the technical support requirements needed for any proposed plan.

PHASE 2: SHELFLIST ANALYSIS

Goal: To identify, describe, and document existing shelflist files and standardize the data they contain.

Tasks:

1. Institute quality control measures to assure consistency of entries within the file.
2. Undertake an inventory of the collection.
3. Verify existing bibliographic information in the shelflist records.
4. Locate and add missing bibliographic information to the records.
5. Implement uniform standardized cataloging practices and consistent use of cutter numbers.

PHASE 3: RETROSPECTIVE CONVERSION

Goal: To implement a program of retrospectively converting the library's manual bibliographic database.

Tasks:

1. Prepare protocols for bibliographic and item standards.
2. Organize staff for an in-house retrospective conversion effort, or,
3. Prepare and distribute Requests for Proposal (RFP) or Bid (RFB) for a vendor-supplied retrospective conversion.
4. Evaluate vendor responses and select a vendor.

PHASE 4: SYSTEM SPECIFICATIONS/REQUIREMENTS

Goal: To prepare and distribute an RFP/B, with specifications, for an automated system.

Tasks:

1. Write specifications for a system.
2. Incorporate specifications into an RFP/B document.
3. Distribute RFP/B to appropriate vendors of automated systems.

PHASE 5: ANALYZE PROPOSALS/SELECT VENDOR

Goal: To analyze vendor responses to the RFP/B and to select a vendor to implement a system.

Tasks:

1. Evaluate vendor proposals.
2. Communicate with vendors for follow-up information.

3. Set up system demonstrations, interviews with vendor clients, and/or visits to existing vendor sites.
4. Select a vendor.

PHASE 6: CONTRACT NEGOTIATIONS

Goal: To negotiate a favorable purchase contract with the selected vendor.

Tasks:

1. Involve legal counsel, together with library personnel, in the drafting and/or evaluation of a contract.
2. Bring negotiations to a successful and favorable conclusion.

PHASE 7: SYSTEM IMPLEMENTATION

Goal: To install the selected system.

Tasks:

1. Customize the vendor's system to the library's policies.
2. Physically prepare the site.
3. Install and test the hardware, software, and telecommunications.
4. Acquire the necessary forms, supplies, and equipment.
5. Load and index library's bibliographic database.
6. Train and re-educate staff; realign workflow and space.
7. Activate and evaluate operation of the system.

5 IDENTIFYING TECHNOLOGICAL OPTIONS FOR AUTOMATION

There are a number of different paths to automation available to libraries. Your challenge will be to identify them and assess their benefits to your library in relation to (1) the priorities that emerged out of your library profile and strategic planning and (2) the cost of these options.

Options include:

- *Enhance or replace an existing system* As more and more libraries reach the end of the life cycle of their first system, they are often migrating to an enhanced version of their current system or to an entirely different system. Hardware and software products have changed drastically in the last few years, so that a system migration will likely result in a total replacement not only of the current hardware and software but also of the cabling and telecommunications equipment. Thus, a needs assessment process resulting in a profile and strategic plan is as vital for a library migrating from one system to another as for a library automating for the first time.

- *Acquire software to run on a computer network already in place* Library software packages are now designed to run on local area networks. If the appropriate hardware, operating system software, and network architecture are already in place, a library may save money by using available hardware resources to run a library system. While this may allow a library to jump relatively painlessly onto the automation bandwagon, it could also tie the library to a system that— though compatible with an existing network—is not entirely suited to its needs.

- *Write software for a system developed in-house* Some institutions may still have data-processing staff that want to write software for a custom-made system designed to run on equipment already available on-site. Given the complexity of library operations and the need for a complex program to handle them, the cost of this option in person hours, time, and computing resources is very substantial, usually prohibitively so. In addition, today's emphasis on systems as gateways to resources outside the library's walls makes writing dedicated in-house software an unsatisfactory solution.

- *Purchase a turnkey system* "Turnkey" refers to commercially available, off-the-shelf systems that house hardware and/or software configurations for library purposes. Turnkey, however, does *not* mean that the system miraculously runs itself without human intervention. The systems shown at conference exhibits or advertised in library journals are, for the most part, turnkey systems. These systems increasingly are designed to run on local and wide area networks that utilize powerful microcomputer servers and personal computer workstations. Speed, capacity, and performance are all determined by the size of the server and by the mix of factors such as functions performed, collection size, and user base. These systems, properly sized, will serve equally well a single library automating one or more functions or an array of libraries performing a multiplicity of functions.

- *Join an existing automated system or network of libraries* Many libraries do not acquire their own system, whether alone or with other libraries, but instead elect to hook up with an already existing automated network of libraries. The decision to do so may stem from such considerations as cost, politics, convenience, or a combination of these.

Measuring the above options against your library profile and the goals and objectives of your strategic plan will likely result in the elimination of one or more alternatives. How best to evaluate the remaining options? Some possibilities include:

- Read about system options in journal articles and in reviews such as those in *Library Technology Reports*
- Visit libraries that have implemented the options that interest you
- Hire a consultant to evaluate each option and its cost implications and to recommend specifically what is appropriate for your library.

ISSUES IN JOINING A CONSORTIUM

Libraries react to joining a consortium in many ways, depending on a host of factors—only one of which is cost. For example, some libraries may have had a negative experience in a previous consortial arrangement. Others may lack a tradition of cooperation or may have a strong history of independent action and decision making. In such instances, a cooperative approach to automation is not an option, regardless of cost considerations.

Typically, however, cost considerations loom large in the planning process, and a library must carefully identify the costs associated with any automation option. Indeed, for a smaller library, automation may seem overwhelming and out of reach because of the costs involved. For this reason, many libraries seek to automate jointly with other libraries or to become part of an existing system.

The shared expense of togetherness may or may not represent a savings for the individual library. For example, sharing the purchase of a large, complex network that accommodates a great number of users may mean that an individual library's costs will be greater than if the library were to automate independently. Similarly, joining an existing system may cost as much as purchasing a system locally because the system is likely to pass along the costs of adding a new member to the joining library.

Bear in mind, though, that a library's mix of collection size, user base, and activity levels may require that it acquire hardware that, in terms of initial cost, may exceed the costs of a joint venture. Plus, when you add indirect costs (such as staff time) to direct costs (such as purchase price and ongoing expenses), a cooperative approach often proves more cost effective than going it alone.

In essence, deciding whether to join a consortium of libraries is complicated and requires a detailed examination of all the elements that are associated with automating a library operation.

AN EXAMPLE OF A FUNDING FORMULA FOR CONSORTIA

In this model, library members of a consortia decide upon annual target goals to fund their anticipated needs. Then an assessment is developed based upon these target goals, with each participating member assessed cost shares according to the following formula:

Member share	25 percent of the target, divided by the number of participating libraries
Site share	25 percent of the target, divided by the number of participating library sites
Port share	50 percent of the target, divided by the number of active ports

A library pays the member share x 1, the site share x 1 or more (for a branch or branches), and the port share x the number of ports it is using on the system.

Note: Integrated library systems now often operate on PC workstations connected to a local area network (LAN) with just the server plugged into a port. This is a change from earlier environments, in which "dumb" terminals were plugged into the Central Processing Unit (CPU) through individual ports. As a result, the concept of the "port share" becomes less viable because there are few ports in use in the traditional sense.

Possible alternatives to the port share might be a fee structure based on the size of the local area network in which the number of workstations connected to the network is used to calculate the share cost. This might be refined further so that workstations dedicated solely to the library system would be assessed at a full share rate, while workstations utilized primarily for other functions would be assessed at a partial rate.

ILLUSTRATION

For purposes of this illustration, assume 20 participating libraries and 35 sites with a total of 400 workstations. *Participation* means any library or group of libraries accessing the automated system for whatever purpose. The *measure* of participation is not the level of activity, number of functions accessed, or services utilized. Rather, it is the *number of ports* used by that library or group of libraries.

Assume a target goal of *$500,000*. Thus:

Member share (25%): $125,000/20 libraries = $6,250/library
Site share (25%): $125,000/35 sites = $3,571/site
Port share (50%): $250,000/400 ports = $625/port

Figure 5–1 illustrates how the assessments would work for three consortium members, where Public Library A is a single library with no branches using 12 ports; Public Library B is one library with one branch site using 20 ports; and Group of Libraries is a group with four members using 50 ports.

Figure 5–1 Allocation of Consortium Assessment			
	Public Library A	**Public Library B**	**Group of Libraries**
Participant share	$6,250.00	$6,250.00	$6,250.00
Site share	$3,571.00	$7,142.00	$14,284.00
Port share	$7,500.00	$12,500.00	$31,250.00
Total assessment:	**$17,321.00**	**$25,892.00**	**$51,784.00**

SOURCES

Agnew, Grace, and Toni Lambert. *Online System Migration Guide* (LITA Monographs 7). Chicago: Library and Information Technology Association/American Library Association, 1996.

This 47-page guide offers a "practical checklist for online system migration." Four sections cover data preparation for export, hardware and facilities preparation (including telecommunications), preparing library staff, and vendor support issues.

Boss, Richard W. *The Library Manager's Guide to Automation.* 3d ed. Boston: G.K. Hall, 1990.

This book includes a review of six system procurement options (chapter 6) and also discusses issues involved in costing automated systems (chapter 8).

Cortez, Edwin M., and Tom Smorch. *Planning Second Generation Automated Library Systems.* Westport, CT: Greenwood, 1993.

A summary of the experience that librarians have gained from prior computerization. There are chapters on hardware and software, special automation needs, and networking and connectivity issues.

6 TRANSLATING NEEDS AND PRIORITIES INTO SPECIFICATIONS FOR NETWORKED SYSTEMS

DESIGNING SPECIFICATIONS

Once you have determined your needs and prioritized them, it is time to think about what you want your automated system to do for you. Here, you are interested in the *whats*, not the *hows*. Just as you do not have to know how cruise control works in order to know what it does for you as you drive down the highway, you do not have to understand the inner workings of an automated system in order to verbalize what you want out of it.

You have already documented the processes that occur within each library function. Now you must break these down into specifications, which are what you want your automated system to do, including things that your existing system, whether automated or manual, cannot do.

In essence, specifications define the capabilities that you want in a system. Specify and prioritize attributes ranging from the required (if it's not there, you won't buy the system) to the desirable (nice to have, but you can live without it). Specifications also cover technical areas such as standards that must be adhered to, system operation, maintenance, and system and data security.

Developing clear and accurate specifications that are particular to your library is one of the most important, if not *the* most important, activity you will engage in as you plan for your automated system. These specifications will carry you through the entire procurement process. The system that most closely matches them will be the most useful and the most responsive to your needs.

A Sample Specifications Checklist appears in Figure 6–1.

Figure 6–1 Sample Specifications Checklist

GENERAL SPECIFICATIONS
1. The system must be a real-time, graphical, open, distributed client/server system.
2. The system design must be object oriented with distributed objects.
3. The system must be written in a common programming language and utilize a recognized processing standard.
4. The system must provide seamless, flexible, nonmodular functionality emphasizing streamlined, simple work flows between functional processes.
5. Information, including bibliographic, must be exportable and importable in multiple formats and in both merged and separate files. The system must support global replace and change across all functional processes.
6. The system must have the ability to provide a full recovery from any type of system failure through back-up or data redundancy.
7. The system must allow for the addition of workstations and the expansion of features without requiring major system redesign or replacement of hardware.
8. The system must include a methodology for offline operations for user services and access.
9. The system must function in an inter-networking environment through local, wide, and/or metropolitan area networks, with access to the Internet and the World Wide Web utilizing broadband network services.
10. The system must support remote access through both dial-up telephone lines and online networks.

FUNCTIONAL PROCESSES

User Access
1. The system must support a graphical user interface that is common to both on-site and remote users.
2. The system must support multiple search modes geared to the user's proficiency and skill, including a search mode designed for children.
3. The system must support multiple locally stored databases, such as a materials database and a community information database.
4. The system must support and retain customized personal profiles and preferences for individuals, including screen layout, search histories, and current awareness search strategies.
5. The system must support individual, protected access to user-specific information.
6. The system must provide the capability for individual users to perform unmediated services, such as placement of reserves and interlibrary loan requests, and to interact with document delivery services, either fee-based or subsidized.
7. The system must support the linkages required to seamlessly search, with one search command, simultaneous, multiple databases located on-site and/or at remote locations.

8. The system must provide online searching aids, such as spell checkers, dictionaries, and thesauri.
9. The system must support the use of automated helpers and online aids to assist in search refinement.
10. The system must support natural language searching, relevancy ranking of searches, and the use of controlled authorized vocabulary.
11. The system must support printing, downloading, and exporting of search results to disk files, paper, or into other software applications.
12. The system must support seamless linkages with databases and tools running on CD-ROM and multimedia servers.
13. The system must support the use of the system by the physically challenged.
14. The system must provide customized management reports on user access to the system.

User Services
1. The system must support the circulation of materials, including charge, check-in, renewal, and holds for users through direct borrowing or intra-/inter-library loan.
2. The system must support the creation and circulation management of collections tailored for specific user needs, such as reserve rooms, bookmobiles, rental or rotating circuit collections, collections delivered to shut-ins, and media scheduling and distribution.
3. The system must support the generation of both defined and customized (utilizing a report program generator) reports and notices for both public and staff users. All reports must be available through screen display, in hard copy, and via e-mail.
4. The system must support the registration and management of users, including delinquencies, blocks, fines, receipt generation, and updating of patron information.

Materials Management
1. The system must support the full MARC II standard, and all USMARC bibliographic records and associated formats, holdings, authorities, and bibliographic and data element standards. These include US/MARC/ALA character sets; non-Roman/CJK (Chinese/Japanese/Korean) character sets; and other formats such as HTML, SGML, GIF, JPEG, Java, and/or ActiveX.
2. The system must support major authorities and thesauri—including Library of Congress Name and Subject Authorities, Medical Subject Headings, and Sears—as well as major classification systems such as DDC, LC, and SuDoc.
3. The system must support import and export of bibliographic records from all major bibliographic utilities, for example, OCLC, BiblioFile, LaserQuest, RLG, SuperCat, Marcive, and the like.
4. The system must support the seamless creation and linkage of item information.
5. The system must support full editing of all the information stored in the catalog records.

6. The system must support the ability to utilize data within the catalog record (e.g., a Uniform Resource Locator (URL)) to hyperlink to and access hardcopy, electronic, and multimedia materials, both locally and remotely stored.
7. The system must provide a linkage between journal titles owned by the library and journal titles cited in citation databases.
8. The system must support the electronic procurement of materials, the verification of order data, linkages between order records and fund accounts, and multiple order types, including blanket and standing orders, and deposit accounts.
9. The system must support the receipt, invoicing, and check-in of materials, including periodicals, standing orders, and bindery returns.
10. The system must track and generate claims for materials or issues not received.
11. The system must generate reports, both predefined and customized, that cover all statistical and management aspects of the control of materials, their purchase, receipt, processing, and use.
12. The system must support a fund accounting system that tracks and accounts for materials expenditures.

STANDARDS

1. The system must conform to full MARC II standard and support all USMARC formats, including bibliographic, authorities, and holdings.
2. The system must comply with applicable NISO standards.
3. The system must accommodate the full ASCII and US/MARC/ALA character sets.
4. The system must support the *Anglo-American Cataloguing Rules*, 2d edition, revised.
5. The system must support appropriate communications and electrical standards and protocols.

Security

1. The system must provide security to prevent accidental or unauthorized modification of records.
2. The system must include safeguards that make it impossible for any person using a workstation to destroy an entire file.
3. The system must provide tiered, password-controlled structures of authorization for applications and operations use that are independent of each other.
4. The system must produce hard-copy notices of items held by borrowers; notices must be printed so that no borrower information is visible.
5. The system must retain no historical record of items borrowed by an individual once the items have been returned and all exceptional conditions have been cleared.

PLANNING NETWORKED SYSTEMS

New developments are changing how automated library systems are designed and constructed. As a result, libraries can no longer plan or design specifications for self-contained systems. They must evaluate and choose systems that connect with other systems to provide gateways to information. *All libraries, not just consortia and libraries with remote sites, must plan networked systems.*

INTRODUCTION

In the past, only libraries with branches or those linked in consortial arrangements worried about networking, especially telecommunications equipment and telephone connections required to connect remote terminals to the host computer. However, local area networks (LANs) that allow users to share files, printers, and other resources such as CD-ROMs have become more common in libraries. It has also become more common for libraries to be connected to organization-wide LANs so that library services can be accessed remotely from users' desktop computers.

At the same time, remote access to global information resources has assumed new importance. Automated library systems operating on LANs are becoming more common, displacing the traditional systems running on host mainframe, minicomputer, or supermicrocomputers. Many of these systems are employing client/server architecture in which a client requests services and a server computer provides them. Unlike the hierarchical computer (host)/dumb terminal (slave) model, a given computer may function as both client and server, may connect to multiple servers and clients simultaneously, and may operate on different computer platforms.

Note that the distribution of tasks among clients and servers is handled in a variety of different ways. Some systems may retain the bulk of the activity on the server, with the client workstations only assuming a small part of the processing responsibility. Other systems may distribute the workload so that the workstations take on more of the processing responsibility. When this happens, the distinction between the server and the workstation becomes blurred. While many systems still employ the more centralized architecture—not much different from the old host/slave model— the trend is more toward distributed, object-oriented processing, in which a machine functions as both server and client.

LOCAL AREA NETWORKS

A result of this trend is that library automation vendors are no longer supplying the peripheral hardware and the telecommunications equipment and cabling needed to run their systems, even when the library is self-contained at a single site. The creation of the network architecture and the telecommunications connections is now becoming the library's responsibility, and the library is often encouraged to purchase this equipment locally.

The first step, then, in planning a networked system, is to create a local area network in your library. This can be done before a system has been selected, but it is very important to adhere to the cabling and networking standards listed in chapter 15 so that most vendors' automated library systems will run on it.

Libraries developing LANs should select hardware and software that are likely to be compatible with the widest possible range of systems and applications. The best options for use with a library automation system (as well as other applications) are:

- as many network-ready personal computers with as much storage, speed, cache, and random access memory as the budget allows
- Ethernet network architecture
- Category 5 unshielded twisted pair (UTP) cable supporting data transmission rates (bandwidth) of up to 100 megabytes per second.
- Unix, Netware, or Windows NT/95 network operating system.

HANDY HINT	
	Hire experienced data cable installers instead of electricians to install the cable wire and terminate the connections. Improperly installed and terminated cable will adversely affect your network's operation.

INTER-NETWORKS

Once you have installed a LAN, it can be extended or connected to other networks in a remote environment by using longer cable runs, if the distance is short, or by using an outside telecommunications provider, if the distance is greater.

When LANs in remote locations are connected together, they become wide area or metropolitan networks, the best known of which is the Internet. These networks require higher speed lines with greater bandwidth because more data is passing through them over a greater distance.

Telecommunications options for these networks include:

- frame relay
- switched multimegabit data service (SMDS)
- asynchronous transfer mode (ATM).

In order to offer a full range of information services to users at optimum speeds, all libraries, and especially consortia and large systems, must compare competing broadband network service options carefully, paying particular attention to:

- local availability
- price
- minimum bandwidth and speed guarantees.

CONCLUSION

Every library, regardless of size or location, must address these issues in order to connect to the Internet and access the brave new world of Web-based public catalogs and external databases, which contain text, images, and full-motion video. This access is the pay-off for the effective design and implementation of networked systems. Careful planning when initally installing local area and wide area networks and adherence by both library and vendor to specified standards ensures an exciting and valuable inter-networking experience for both libraries and users.

SOURCES

Boss, Richard W. "Facilities Planning for Technology." *Library Technology Reports* 31:4 (July–August 1995), 393–483.

The author considers book storage, work space planning, and information technology from the perspective of library facilities planning. Of special interest are the sections on automated library systems (pp. 416–422) and on cabling, LANs, and networks (pp. 439–456), which offer useful, nontechnical definitions of networking jargon.

Cooper, Michael D. *Design of Library Automation Systems: File Structures, Data Structures, and Tools.* New York: Wiley, 1996.

"The purpose of this book is to give the reader an understanding of the structure of library automation systems with . . . information about underlying algorithms, file structures, and processing strategies."
Part 1 covers organizational and managerial problems of library automation and includes a description of the file structure and design of OPAC, circulation, acquisition, and serials modules. Part 2 examines file-management tools needed to build library automation systems as well as MARC record management. Part 3 discusses procedures that retrieve, browse, display, and edit data, including authority control and client/server system design.

Green, James Harry. *The Irwin Handbook of Telecommunications Management.* 2d ed. Chicago: Irwin Professional, 1996.

This book is a comprehensive how-to manual and hands-on resource dealing with the many facets of managing telecommunications systems. Of special interest are pages 29–38 in chapter 2, which offer a brief review of the current trends in telecommunications; chapter 13 (pp. 278–318), which describes data communications equipment and services (LANs, types of data circuits); and chapters 6 through 8 (pp. 119–172), which discuss developing requirements and specifications, writiing RFPs, and evaluating vendor proposals.

Horak, Ray. *Communications Systems and Networks.* New York: M&T Books, 1997.

According to its cover, this book "demystifies communications systems including voice, data, broadband networks, and convergence technologies." It covers communications network devices and processes (e.g., multiplexers, switches), transmissions (e.g., twisted-pair, fiber optics), digital and data networking (e.g., SMDS, Frame Relay, ATM, ISDN), LANs and Internetworking, WANs and MANs, wireless transport, as well as issues relating to the Internet and the World Wide Web. A discussion of regulation issues and the impact of the Telecommunications Act of 1996 is also included.

Howden, Norman. *Local Area Networking for the Small Library: A How-To-Do-It Manual for Librarians.* 2d ed. New York: Neal-Schuman, 1997.

"Offers clear guidance on every aspect of LAN from start-up through maintenance and trouble shooting." An installation checklist and a user-needs analysis are also included.

Meghabghab, Dania Bilal. *Automating Media Centers and Small Libraries: A Microcomputer-Based Approach.* Englewood, CO: Libraries Unlimited, 1997.

"The author compares various library functions within the automated and unautomated environments," describes system selection and implementation, and offers guidelines for needs assessments and functions analysis. She also treats topics that will be discussed in subsequent sections of *this* book, including RFP preparation, bar coding and database maintenance, MARC/MicroLIF, and the Z39.50 standard.

7 TURNING YOUR SPECIFICATIONS INTO A REQUEST FOR VENDOR PROPOSALS

Once you have determined what you want an automated system to do for you and have translated your needs into specifications, you are ready to begin the actual process of procuring a system. If you are in a public institution, you are subject to a bevy of public laws that require purchases of this type to be offered publicly in a competitive manner. This may mean that you will have to go through a formal procurement process in order to acquire your system.

PREPARING THE RFP

In many cases, public institutions are able to issue *Requests for Proposal* (RFP) instead of *Requests for Bid* (RFB). An RFB implies a very restrictive procurement requiring the library to negotiate with the bidder who meets the minimum requirements at the lowest cost. Procurements based on RFPs are generally preferable to those based on RFBs because you can consider noncost factors such as the overall suitability of the system. Your local purchasing regulations will stipulate how you must proceed.

If yours is not a public institution, you may feel that you can skip this entire process. While you are not legally bound to issue an RFP/RFB, it is still in your best interest to undertake an RFP process. Releasing an RFP and requiring vendors to respond to it in a standardized fashion allows you to compare products in a systematic and methodical manner.

It is very difficult to compare systems sensibly and pragmatically solely by viewing vendor demonstrations, talking to sales representatives, reading literature, or comparing broad cost quotations. Using an RFP to solicit written responses allows you to compare functionality, cost, maintenance, support, and all the other issues that are involved in system procurements. The process can save you money and will, in all likelihood, result in a wiser decision.

Your specifications form the basis of your RFP/RFB. If you are preparing an RFB, much of the language will be dictated by your local purchasing authorities. You should, however, be able to insert your specifications in the appropriate spots in the document.

The rest of this chapter presents an outline of an RFP for an online, integrated, automated system. As with the specifications, your RFP should be tailored to your own situation; for example, if you are purchasing software only, then you will have shorter sections on hardware.

Figures 7–1 through 7–4 show additional sample forms you might append to the RFP. These include:

- *Notice of Intent to Respond Form*, used by a prospective vendor to inform the library that a proposal is forthcoming (Figure 7–1)
- *System Specification Response Form*, a sample page from the RFP listing specifications (in this instance for the cataloging function)—for libraries wishing to include this level of detail—to which the vendor must respond indicating availability (Figure 7–2)
- *Equipment List Form*, onto which the vendor is asked to list equipment required for the system; the form should request information on hardware (principally, servers and workstations), peripherals (e.g., printers), telecommunications, software, vendor services (e.g., database conversion services), and supplies (Figure 7–3)
- *Price Quotation Form*, where the vendor is to list prices for the items on the Equipment List Form (Figure 7–4).

Figure 7–1 Notice of Intent to Respond Form

Please fill out and return this form no later than _____
                                                                    (date and time)

Name of Company Responding
to Proposal: _____

Name of Contact Person: _____

Telephone Number of
Contact Person: _____

Signature of Representative
of Company _____

CONFIDENTIAL

Figure 7–2 System Specification Response Form

CATALOGING AND BIBLIOGRAPHIC MAINTENANCE REQUIREMENTS

Bibliographic Database

Bibliographic records in full MARC II format, including all MARC fields, both fixed and variable, and all MARC bibliographic and holdings formats, must be supported.

_____

Note: The vendor must provide, as an attachment and referencing this specification, a list of the names of all the bibliographic utilities from which MARC records are currently being successfully loaded into the system (hereafter referred to as "said utilities").

The system must accept and be able to accommodate the loading of MARC tapes as formatted by said utilities through tape, disk, or online electronic transfer.

_____

The system must have an interface for said utilities for the transfer of bibliographic records.

_____

The aforementioned interfaces must transfer the entire MARC record, including all of the fixed fields and leader into the system.

_____

The aforementioned interfaces must trap duplicate records corresponding to those already in the system's database and send the duplicates to a suspend file for manual review and disposition.

_____

FIGURE 7–3 Equipment List Form

SYSTEM HARDWARE

Item	Quantity	Model/Manufacturer	Functional Description

Figure 7–4 Price Quotation Form

SYSTEM HARDWARE

Item	Quantity	Unit Cost	Total Cost	Maintenance	Annual Lease-Purchase Price

TOTAL

OUTLINE FOR REQUEST FOR PROPOSALS FOR AN ONLINE, AUTOMATED, INTEGRATED LIBRARY SYSTEM

INTRODUCTION

Background Information on the Library
1. Statement of purpose regarding automation.
2. Narrative profile of the library (e.g., collection size, circulation, patron count).

General Rules and Conditions for Submission
1. Overview (library's automation goals and objectives).
2. Schedule of activities (timeline for project).
3. Submission of proposals
    a. Number of copies to be submitted and to whom
    b. Due date
    c. Due date for submission of Notice of Intent to Respond Form (see Figure 7–1).

Proposal Format
1. Arrangement
    a. Responses must follow RFP's format and enumeration.
    b. Required forms must be utilized, filled out, and returned.
    c. Specified standard descriptors must be used (see below for examples).
    d. User and/or systems operation documentation must accompany proposal (specify number of copies).
    e. Marketing and technical literature and other reference materials may accompany proposal, but must be packaged separately from the response.
    f. Vendors must respond to all functional, technical, and performance requirements in the RFP, and responses must be understood without reference to other documents.
2. Standardized descriptors (to be used to respond to functional and technical specifications and other requirements and specifications as appropriate):
    * "In general release"—in production at all user sites (indicate number of sites). If the function is available always at all user sites and some users choose not to use this function, consider the function in general release.
    * "In testing"—in testing and evaluation either in-house and/or at user sites. Indicate the expected date for general release.

- "In design"—in detailed definition, design, programming, etc. Indicate expected date for general release.
- "In planning"—in general requirements definition or early planning. Indicate expected dates for design, testing, and general release.
- "Not available"—not expected to be a future function or will require special programming at the library's expense to provide.

INSTRUCTIONS TO VENDORS

Letter of Introduction
1. Signed by an officer of the firm.
2. Name and address of the firm.
3. Name, address, and phone number of authorized contact.

Vendor's Company
1. Description of company organization and staffing.
2. Resumes of key staff.

Vendor's Financial Stability
1. Audited financial statement for past five years or as many years as company has been in business (if less than five).
2. Access to Dun and Bradstreet report if available.
3. Credit references.

Management Summary (brief statement of system features)

Qualifications of Vendors
1. Client list.
2. Right to visit sites.

Signatures
1. Submission with signatures of appropriate company officers.
2. Corrections and erasures initialed by person signing the proposal or authorized representative.

Proposal Evaluation
1. Scoring criteria:
    a. Compliance with specifications set forth in RFP
    b. Adequacy of hardware configuration
    c. Availability of all desired software modules
    d. Functionality (workflows between functional processes)
    e. Capability for system expansion and upgrading
    f. Cost
    g. Maintenance and support
    h. Training
    i. Documentation
    j. Vendor's past performance

k. Vendor's financial and organizational credibility
l. Overall suitability of the system.
2. Proposals evaluated in the same manner.

Withdrawal of Proposals
1. Instructions for withdrawal prior to opening of proposals.

Inquiries/Vendors' Conference
1. Instructions for vendor inquiries and/or scheduling of a vendors'/bidders' conference.

Reserved Rights and Special Requirements (will generally be supplied by purchasing or legal department and will vary depending on whether procurement is a proposal or a bid).

TRAINING AND DOCUMENTATION

Training
1. Levels and types of training provided.
2. Description of training program, including trainers, qualifications, methodologies, and schedules.
3. Types of staff for whom training must be provided (computer operators, supervisors and administrators, public services and technical services (staff).

Documentation
1. Number of copies of user and system manuals that should be part of system purchase.
2. Types of documentation required.
3. Policies regarding revisions and upgrades.
4. Extent of online help.

SYSTEM SPECIFICATIONS

Vendor must use preformatted response forms and the standardized descriptors described earlier (see Figure 7–2)

Specifications developed by the library

DATABASE CREATION

1. Creation of bibliographic database.
2. Creation of item database.
3. Creation of borrower database.

MAINTENANCE

General Description of Maintenance Services, including
1. Hours of service.
2. Turnaround time.
3. Availability of an 800 number to report problems.

4. Availability of dial-in diagnostics.
5. Types of service (on-site, depot, or combination).
6. Nearest hardware service location and number of service personnel and field engineers assigned to it.
7. Size of local parts inventory.
8. Cost of service including premium rates, if any, for off-hours service.

Preventive maintenance program offered

Provisions for activation and termination of maintenance

Maintenance Costs
1. Server hardware maintenance requirements.
2. Software maintenance requirements.
3. Peripheral devices maintenance requirements.

DELIVERY AND INSTALLATION SCHEDULING AND SITE PREPARATION

Description of delivery and installation methodologies

Description of system site preparation requirements

WARRANTIES

(Warranties should be determined in conjunction with local purchasing and legal departments.)

COST PROPOSAL

Vendor must utilize Equipment List and Price Quotation Forms provided with RFP (see Figures 7–3 and 7–4)

Financial alternatives (purchase, lease, lease-purchase)

Prices and price protection (these should be determined in conjunction with local purchasing and legal departments)

APPENDICES

1. Library's current and projected (five years) file statistics (e.g., title/item count, number of borrowers).
2. Library's current and projected activity statistics (e.g., circulation, new acquisitions, new borrowers).
3. Estimates of the location and number of workstations.
4. Library operating hours.
5. Library address and telephone/fax numbers.

SOURCES

Boss, Richard W. "The Procurement of an Automated Library System." *Library Technology Reports* 30:3 (May–June 1994), 331–440.

"This issue presents an updated and refined model or sample RFP (Request for Proposal) for an online integrated library system." The earlier report on this subject was published in the September/October 1990 issue (26:5).

Cortez, Edwin M. *Proposals and Contracts for Library Automation.* Studio City, CA: Pacific Information, 1987. *Out of print.*

Describes how to draft and evaluate RFPs for library automation, as well as how to negotiate with automation vendors. The procurement process is reviewed.

Reader, Evan A. "Competitive Procurement of Integrated Library Systems." *Library Hi Tech* 7:2 (Issue 26, 1989), 7–15.

"The procurements (at California State University) demonstrated that competitive bidding not only is highly effective in reducing the overall cost of library systems, but also allows the buyer to achieve favorable contract provisions that would be difficult if not impossible to obtain in a noncompetitive environment."

Wilkinson, Frances C., and Connie Capers Thorson. *The RFP Process: Effective Management of the Acquisition of Library Materials.* Englewood, CO: Libraries Unlimited, forthcoming.

This book "shows librarians how to successfully prepare RFPs when determining which vendors to use for purchasing library materials." There is "specific information on electronic/automated services."

3 EVALUATING PROPOSALS

MAKING THE FIRST CUT

Once you have received vendor proposals, it is time to begin the process of system evaluation and selection. The first step is to form a project team to assist you—people who have some knowledge of automation or who work in the area(s) being automated.

You will have read some articles, stopped by vendor booths in exhibit halls, and perhaps requested literature and general cost information from vendors whose products look interesting—*but it is the RFP or RFB that will be the cornerstone of your evaluation process*. Thus, if possible, try to wait until you have received all or most vendor responses to your RFP/RFB and have had the opportunity to give them an initial look-through before taking the next step, which is to schedule system demonstrations. By so doing, you will avoid having to look at a system that is eliminated early in the evaluation process either because the vendor chose not to respond or because the response was "fatally flawed."

Responses can be fatally flawed for a number of reasons:

- Sections or conditions required by legal or purchasing regulations may be missing or unmet.
- Critical sections of the document may not have been responded to—for example, the vendor did not reply to any of the technical specifications.
- For a software only purchase, the RFP/B may have specified that the system must run on specific hardware and the vendor's software cannot.
- The system may be missing the applications module for a specific library function that is your number-one priority.

Problems such as these immediately eliminate a system from further consideration. It is critical, however, to be absolutely sure that the flaw is a fatal one before using it to eliminate a vendor from consideration at the outset, particularly in a bid process. If there is any doubt expressed at all from anyone involved in the selection process, it is better not to eliminate the system. Once any fatally flawed responses have been removed, it is time to schedule system demonstrations and begin in-depth reading of the remaining proposals.

HINTS FOR VIEWING SYSTEM DEMONSTRATIONS

1. Request that high priority modules be demonstrated first.
2. Request the display of a tagged, full MARC record.
3. Be alert for, and note, functions or operations that cannot be demonstrated.
4. Ask if the version that is being demonstrated, *for each module*, is the same as the version in current release—that it's what you would be getting if you bought the system.
5. Watch for cumbersome or awkward operations within or between functions.
6. Request that, in addition to the preplanned demonstration scenarios, a few specific searches, operations, etc., be performed that are analogous to real situations in your library. Ask each vendor to perform the same specific operations, so that there will be a common basis of comparison.
7. Take note of specifics about the system's functionality that you judge to be particularly strong, as well as those that appear weak.
8. Telecommunications problems with dial-ups and/or lack of expertise on the part of the demonstrator may hamper the effectiveness of the demonstration. Note this separately from any functionality weaknesses.

SYSTEM DEMONSTRATIONS

Demonstrations are an important component of the evaluation process. You must therefore make the demonstrations as objective as possible and make it as easy as possible for those participating to be able to compare the different systems being demonstrated.

Each vendor has a standard canned demonstration that is meant to show off the system in the most attractive light, highlighting its strengths and camouflaging its weaknesses. It is in your best interest, of course, to see demonstrations that expose the warts as well as the jewels. To do so, allow the demonstration to proceed, then bring out your list of what you want to see demonstrated along with questions you would like answered. It is best to have your lists prepared in advance, and to *use the same lists with each vendor*. Again, this allows you to compare more easily how the systems work as well as how they look and feel. Additional questions will probably arise during each demonstration, and will vary with each vendor, making them less easy to compare. That's okay, as long as your preset questions are answered as well.

It is important that at least some of the same people attend all of the demonstrations. If too many people in your evaluation group have not seen all of the systems, it will be difficult to compare them effectively. Also remember that a number of negatives unrelated to the system's performance can affect a demonstration. A nonworking phone line or an inexperienced sales representative can result in a disappointing demonstration of what may in reality be a good system for your needs. Demonstrations are an important part of the evaluation process, but they should always be kept in perspective and should not be the overriding reason for selecting or eliminating a system.

ANALYZING VENDOR RESPONSES

By far the most time will be spent analyzing the vendors' written responses. Now is the time to sit down with the RFP/B and each response.

- Have pencil and paper or your notebook computer handy.
- Carefully read every response and note any deviations from the requirements as defined by the RFP/B.
- Note any aspect that is handled unusually well.
- Make a list of any parts of the response that are not clear. These will eventually be turned into a list of written questions to which each vendor will be required to respond in writing.

COSTS

The cost portion of the response may be the most difficult to analyze. Depending on the complexity of your system and the number of libraries participating, consider the use of a spreadsheet in order to evaluate the cost breakdowns.

Costs may not be what they seem at first glance. It is not uncommon for the vendor that appears to offer the lowest cost to end up being the most expensive. When comparing costs, it is critical that you compare apples to apples. Requiring vendors to use preformatted forms designed by you makes the task somewhat easier, but it may take a fair amount of digging to discover whether the low-cost vendor is indeed providing the same range of service or material as the more expensive ones. Careful analysis is especially crucial in a bid process, where a low bidder can have a distinct edge.

TEAM EVALUATION

As noted, it is helpful to have more than one person evaluating the responses. You will want to set up a proposal evaluation team if you have not already done so by this time. Request multiple sets of the proposal itself; however, single copies of manuals, documentation, sample contracts, and the like are sufficient. Make sure that your purchasing and legal departments have their own copies of all needed materials.

CALLING VENDOR CLIENTS

Before actually beginning to evaluate the proposals, you will want to call some of each vendor's current clients. The easiest way to have this information at your fingertips is to ask each vendor to provide a client list that includes library type, collection size, size of borrower file, circulation volume, the name of the system, its hardware and, if appropriate, network configuration, and the software applications being used.

Be selective in deciding which clients to contact. Call sites of the same library type(s), and of similar size, where the hardware and software modules that have been proposed to you are *currently* in use. As with the vendor demonstrations, it is important to have a list of questions ready in advance so that the same questions are asked of each site that is called. (See the sample Vendor Client Question List in Figure 8–1.)

SITE CALL HINTS

1. From the list of references supplied by each vendor, choose sites that have the following characteristics:
   - title, item, and patron file sizes and circulation figures similar to your library
   - a shared system (if your system is for a consortium of libraries)
   - a location within your geographic area.
2. Calls should be made to installed, operational sites—not to sites with installations pending.
3. Try to speak with the system manager or automation project coordinator. In most cases, this will not be the director.
4. Explain that you have a number of questions, so that the call may take some time. Encourage short, concise answers, but really informative answers may require some detail.
5. A fair, unbiased survey is guaranteed by asking each site called all of the questions on the list.
6. There is a lot to find out, and the calls will require an investment of time. Keep in mind, however, that these calls are taking the place of formal site visits, which would be even more time-consuming.

Figure 8–1 Vendor Client Question List

Date_____

Library_____

Vendor/System_____

Contact_____

Telephone #_____

1. Describe the system's configuration:

   Telecommunications/network structure _____

   Server _____ Amt./memory _____ Amt./disk storage _____

   No. of installed workstations _____ Functions (cataloging, circulation, OPAC) being used _____

2. What is the size (no. of records) of your:

   Bib. file _____ Item file _____ Borrower file _____
3. What do you like best about the system?
4. What, if anything, would you most like to change in the system?
5. What problems do you have in using the system?
6. How well does the vendor meet time frames for enhancements/new developments/changes?
7. Does the vendor supply good documentation for the system and for upgrades? Have you had any problems with the vendor's new software releases?
8. Is the system user friendly? How easy or hard is it to learn and to train staff and patrons to use it?
9. Is system response time acceptable? Is there deterioration during peak hours of use, during report compilation, or as a result of adding more workstations?
10. Do your vendors respond quickly and effectively to software, hardware, or telecommunications problems?
11. Why did you choose this system?
12. How many staff members run your system? What are their functions? Is the number sufficient?
13. Do you use a gateway to access the Internet, other systems, and/or remote database services? If yes, how effective is it? Is it used by the public directly?
14. Is your vendor providing the appropriate technical assistance you need to establish interfaces with other systems?
15. Can your system export both bibliographic *and* item files in MARC format, integrated in a single bibliographic record? Have you satisfactorily exported bibliographic records and associated item information?

16. What problems, if any, did you encounter during conversion? How did the vendor respond to these or any other problems?
17. Have you applied name and/or subject authority control to your bibliographic file? If yes, what are its strengths and weaknesses? If not, why not?
18. Are your authority records in MARC format? How do you import and export them to and from your system?
19. How many titles and items do you add to your collection per year? What methods do you use to add bibliographic records to your database? Please evaluate their efficiency and effectiveness.
20. Do you use the acquisitions and serials modules? If yes, what are their strengths and weaknesses? Does the serials module include a journal citation function?
21. Do you have the OPAC? Do your users find it easy to use? If not, why not?
22. Does your system have, and are you using, an Information and Referral module? If yes, what are its strengths and weaknesses?
23. Do you get reports through the system? Are you satisfied with them? Are canned reports sufficient, or do you need an optional report generator to get satisfactory reports?

MAKING THE FINAL CUT

Proposals have been read and analyzed, references have been called, and demonstrations have been held. Now it is time to make the final decision.

Members of the evaluation team should gather with the vendor proposals, their notes on demonstrations and telephone calls, and any other information they may have. Plan to spend the day reviewing everything. First, go over the evaluation criteria you outlined for vendors in your RFP and assign each criterion a point value. (See the sample Vendor Proposal Scoring Sheet in Figure 8–2.) The total number of points may equal more than 100. The highest point value should be given to "overall suitability of the system," since it encompasses all aspects of the system. The other criteria should be weighted based on their relative importance.

The team then assigns a score to each criterion for which each system is being evaluated. All of the information that has been derived from the proposals, the demonstrations, and the customer calls must be considered in making these decisions. Some scores will be assigned quickly; others will require much discussion and debate before a consensus is reached.

When each system has received scores for each criterion, total the individual scores to determine the system's final score. The

Figure 8–2 Vendor Proposal Scoring Sheet

CRITERIA	Point Value	VENDORS			
		# 1	# 2	# 3	# 4
Compliance with RFP specifications	(05)				
Adequacy of hardware configuration	(10)				
Availability of desired functional processes	(10)				
Functionality (workflow between functional processes)	(10)				
Capability for system expansion	(10)				
Cost	(10)				
Maintenance and support	(10)				
Functionality	(10)				
Training	(05)				
Documentation	(05)				
Vendor's past performance	(10)				
Vendor's financial/organizational credibility	(05)				
Overall suitability of the system	(20)				
TOTALS	(120)				

system with the highest score becomes the number one finalist, the system with the second highest score is number two, and so on.

Using this scoring technique brings a strong dose of objectivity into what is a very subjective process and works best in an RFP situation. In a bid process, cost is the overriding factor, and low bid can become the most important and highly weighted criterion.

A word to the wise: To maintain a negotiating edge, it is better to cut to two vendors rather than one. If that is impossible, maintain the illusion of competition anyway. Remember, the selection process is not over until the contract is signed. Until that point, never let any vendors know that they have been eliminated, including those with fatal flaws. (Some vendors may badger you for information. Simply tell them that the selection process is continuing and that no final decision has been made.)

This process is not unlike a job search. Candidates are not sent rejection letters until the final candidate has accepted the offer and has been officially hired. The same is true of automation vendors. Until one has been officially chosen and everyone has signed on the dotted line, do not burn your bridges by rejecting the others. If negotiations with your first-choice vendor fall through, you may want to be able to approach your second and third choices.

SOURCES

"Annual Survey of PC- and Mac-Based Library System Vendors." *Library Systems Newsletter* 16:5 (May 1996), 33–42. Also: "International Survey of Automated Library System Vendors: Integrated, Multi-User, Multi-Function Systems Running on Mainframes, Minis, and Micros that Use a Multi-User Operating System." *Library Systems Newsletter* 16:3/4 (March and April 1996), 17–32.

"Each year *LSN* surveys the library automation industry to get an overview of the market and to facilitate comparison among vendors." *Library Systems Newsletter* is produced monthly by *Library Technology Reports*, which "provides critical evaluations of products and systems used in libraries, media centers, schools and other educational instituions." Both *LTR* and the *Newsletter* are published by the American Library Association.

Barry, Jeff, et. al. "Automated System Marketplace 1996: Jockeying for Supremacy in a Networked World." *Library Journal*, 121:6 (April 1, 1996), 40–52.

LJ reviews the library automation marketplace each April. The 1996 analysis focuses on the "unprecedented demand for information access and networking capabilities." These annual reviews describe major vendor products and initiatives, offer sales and market-share information, and discuss general trends in the area of library automation.

Cibbarelli, Pamela R., comp. and ed. *Directory of Library Automation Software, Systems and Services*. Medford, NJ: Information Today, Inc., 1996.

"This publication . . . includes basic information to locate and and compare available options for library automation based on various criteria such as hardware requirements, operating systems, components and applications, and price." The emphasis of this directory is on providing descriptive profiles of software products, retrospective conversion services, online database services, CD-ROM and portable database distributors, and library automation consultants.

9 PUTTING YOUR SYSTEM INTO PLACE

Now that you have completed the selection process and decided on a vendor and a system, there are a few steps you must take before you can have your system up and running. You and your vendor have to negotiate and sign a contract, and you need to make provisions for system maintenance.

CONTRACT NEGOTIATIONS

The purpose of a contract is simple: to document the expectations and obligations, with accompanying safeguards, of both the library and the vendor. The contract is based on the specifications delineated in the library's Request for Proposal or Request for Bid and the vendor's response to that proposal.

The complexity of the contract will depend upon what you are purchasing. A software-only purchase, intended for a network already in place, may be nothing more than a license agreement similar to those accompanying all such kinds of applications software (e.g., word processing or database software). Such a contract may deal only tangentially with hardware. The purchase of a fully integrated system involving multiple applications, hardware, and telecommunications, however, will result in the most comprehensive of contracts.

WHAT DOES THE CONTRACT DO?

Seldom are the vendor's responses 100 percent in accordance with the library's specifications. Thus, the contract needs to:

- interpret and clarify the differences between a vendor's response and the library's specifications
- formalize pricing and payment schedules
- deal with nonperformance issues and remedies, as well as warranties, vendor bankruptcy, software infringement, and maintenance
- safeguard conformance to any legal requirements necessitated by the library's parent organization or governing board.

CONTRACTS: SOME QUICK DEFINITIONS

These definitions offer a sense of the meaning of certain contract-related legal concepts. Readers are urged to consult legal counsel, standard legal references, or titles cited below for fuller explanations.

Express warranty—any direct affirmation of fact relating to the goods sold, as contained in product descriptions or specifications, demonstrations, contractual provisions, etc.

Implied warranty—that of "merchantability," requiring that goods be of average quality for goods of that type. Also, "fitness for a particular purpose," suggesting that the vendor must provide a product that meets the buyer's particular requirements.

Limited warranty—any warranty that is not a "full warranty" is a "limited warranty."

Liquidated damages—amounts stipulated by the parties to a contract as damages for the breach of that contract. Such damages, to be enforceable, must represent a reasonable effort to estimate *actual* damages.

Merger clause—where the written contract is considered the exclusive agreement between the parties and there is a disclaimer of any prior warranties or representations.

Right to reject—buyer's right to reject equipment not functioning properly within a reasonable time and recover both monies paid and certain damages. Right is modified by seller's right to correct problems in a timely manner.

Right to revoke—buyer's right to revoke initial acceptance of goods because of a latent flaw not discovered until later or because promised remedies to deficiencies are unsuccessful.

It is essential that the contract be thoroughly examined by the library's (or its governing body's) legal counsel. Implied and expressed warranties, liquidated damages, limitations to remedies, and rights to reject and revoke are legal issues that are best handled by someone with legal expertise.

It is the library's responsibility, however, to ensure that library-specific issues are addressed and codified within the contract. The best method to insure this is to draft a tightly written Request for Proposal or Bid and then to make sure that it is included in the contract along with the vendor's response. If the vendor has agreed to provide functionality that is not currently available, this should be clearly spelled out in the contract itself.

Here are a few pointers:

- Make sure that your contract ties up loose ends and avoids ambiguity.

- Your contract should define responsibility and liability for as many important problems or contingencies as you can envision.
- Since no contract can cover every minor contingency, be prepared to deal with minor issues as they come up during implementation.
- Your contract should cover all major risks and the major objectives of your system as you have defined them. In negotiations, don't let any matter pass that is important to you.
- The contract should define responsibilities and protect your rights. Don't use it as a club to extract concessions from your vendor. Remember that the contract is an important element in what should become a productive working relationship.

Keep in mind that although most contract negotiations end successfully, not all proceed smoothly. Talks may break down, positions become intractable. It may be necessary to break off negotiations with the first-ranked vendor and move to the second. Remember: as we stressed in chapter 8, the process is never over until it's over, so don't tell any vendors that they have not been selected until contract negotiations have been completed successfully.

SYSTEM MAINTENANCE

Everyone knows how important maintenance is, especially those of us who have broken down on the interstate at midnight or who have organized a bucket brigade under a leaking roof. There are two types of maintenance: *after-the-fact* and *before-the-fact*. To assure your peace of mind and retain your sanity, you will want to make sure that you avail yourself of both types.

Before-the-fact maintenance, better known as preventive maintenance (PM), should be a part of any maintenance agreement that involves hardware. Just as your car needs periodic check-ups, so do your computers. A combination of preventive maintenance and diagnostic tools, utilized by both the hardware and software vendors, can catch disasters before they occur, thereby minimizing your downtime.

After-the-fact maintenance is also critical and is one area where you really get what you pay for. Most hardware and software maintenance contracts will give you 24 hours a day, 7 days a week,

365 days a year service with two-hour turnaround time—if you are willing to pay for it. Unless you are running an airline reservation system or the Pentagon, however, such comprehensive service will be way over your budget and probably not really necessary.

So . . . *know your site*. If you are a busy public library, it may be worthwhile to pay extra for Saturday service or for service after 5 P.M. Also, know your time zone. If your software vendor is in California and you are in New York, the basic service hours may be 7 A.M. to 6 P.M., Pacific Time. For you, this means 10 A.M. to 9 P.M.

It is helpful if hardware and software maintenance calls can be placed via 800 numbers and if calls can be made at any time of the day or night. It is also helpful if your hardware vendor has an office located close to you and has a number of field engineers, as well as an in-depth parts inventory available locally. Then you won't have to spend three days waiting for the widget to arrive in order for your disk drive to run again.

ON-SITE VERSUS DEPOT SERVICE

It is very important to understand that a great deal of your maintenance service will not occur on-site. Service to your central site server hardware and related peripherals may be on-site, but the rest of your equipment, such as client workstations, keyboards, printers, telecommunications equipment, and bar code wands, will probably be subject to depot service. This means that if something doesn't work, you pack it up, mail it to a service depot, and wait for it to return in working condition.

You will want to examine carefully everything involved with depot service, including who pays for shipping costs and insurance, what the turnaround time is, and the provision, if any, for loaner equipment. If possible, try to get on-site service for workstations, keyboards, and telecommunications equipment, since their loss could compromise your ability to function even minimally. If the vendor cannot or will not offer any options for these other than depot service, check around locally for service bureaus that may be willing to work on your equipment.

All software maintenance will be accomplished via a dial-up telephone line from your vendor's place of business. This is standard operating procedure and works just fine.

SELF-INSURANCE

The question of self-insurance always pops up, particularly from parent organizations looking to save money. On the one hand, service contracts are a necessity for your server hardware and telecommunications equipment: this equipment is too expensive to simply replace every time something breaks, and it may not be that easy to find someone to fix the problem if you don't have a contract.

On the other hand, workstations, and especially keyboards and wands, are significantly less expensive. It may be worthwhile either to set up a fund to finance the purchase of new equipment that is put into service when something breaks down or to pay the time-and-materials charges to have repairs made as needed (rather than buying a service contract in advance). If you decide to go this route, be sure that you determine before the fact who will do the "as-needed" repair work and that they will do it on a time-and-materials basis. This service may be depot or on-site. If it is the latter, you will also have to pay travel charges for the service person.

CONCLUSIONS

It is important to be clear about your system vendor's role in the maintenance process in order to avoid finger-pointing. For example, imagine that your system is down. Upon calling the system vendor and describing your situation, you are told that the problem is with telecommunications (translation: call someone else). But the telecommunications company says that the problem is with the system software, so around it goes. Your contract must contain language that specifically defines the system vendor's responsibility for maintaining operations once the system is installed.

Keep in mind, however, that—given the fact that workstations usually serve multiple purposes—your system may be down for reasons unrelated to the integrated system per se. For example, the local area network itself could be down, and the LAN may not be the responsibility of the automation vendor.

In general, though, effective maintenance arrangements will guarantee that you get the best use out of your system with a minimum amount of downtime. Maintenance specifications should be an integral part of your RFP/B, and all maintenance arrangements, specifications, and prices should be clearly delineated in your contract. When you need it, you really need it, and you don't want the provisions to be vague or unclear.

SOURCES

Bielefield, Arlene, and Lawrence Cheeseman. *Library Contracts and the Law*. New York: Neal-Schuman, forthcoming.

"This volume will help librarians understand, negotiate, and avoid the pitfalls of all kinds of contracts that might be used in libraries. . . . Numerous practical examples, checklists, remedies for breach, and sample contracts for a wide variety of agreements are included."

Cortez, Edwin M., and Edward John Kazlauskas. *Managing Information Systems and Technologies: A Basic Guide for Design, Selection, Evaluation, and Use*. New York: Neal-Schuman, 1986.

Chapter 6 deals with system maintenance and protection.

Spanner, Robert A., and William F. Mack. "Sharpening Your Clause." In Joseph R. Matthews, ed. *A Reader on Choosing an Automated Library System*. Chicago: A.L.A., 1983, 143–149. *Out of print*.

Review of terms and concepts associated with contractual clauses. Covers warranties, mergers, limitation of remedies, reject and revoke clauses.

10 TRAINING! TRAINING! TRAINING!

When thinking of automation planning, there is often a tendency to focus on the hardware and software aspects of planning and to ignore the human aspects of automation—specifically, staff and user training. Without these, the most carefully designed system may not be accepted by library staff or library users. To insure the success of your hard planning work, a training plan should be part of any automation project.

SECRETS OF SUCCESSFUL TRAINING

To insure that your training efforts are as effective as possible, the following training tips should be kept in mind:

1. Designate an individual or group of individuals who will work closely with vendor representatives and will have responsibility for ongoing training.
2. Focus on those skills most relevant to day-to-day operations.
3. Work with small groups and provide hands-on experience.
4. Do practice training on a small test group first.
5. Make sure that trainees can go back and actually use the system immediately after receiving training.
6. Always check your equipment, software, and database prior to beginning training.
7. Ask trainees to evaluate training sessions and make changes accordingly.
8. Offer refresher training on a regular basis.

TRAINING AND RETRAINING STAFF

It is important to remember that when we automate, we are not just learning how to use an automated system; we are in most instances also learning new jobs. Fortunately, training can begin long before the system is installed. By involving staff at all levels in the analysis of operations, the identification of needs, the setting of priorities, the development of specifications, and the evaluation of systems, staff will gain much of the general knowledge they need as the planning progresses.

When developing the RFP, pay particular attention to the section on training:

- Identify and plan your training needs.
- Describe in detail what you expect to receive from the vendor's training program.
- State objectives clearly and ask for a detailed outline of the training offered, including the curriculum, the amount of time spent on each segment, the number of people to be trained at once, and the cost.
- Ask what training aids the vendor provides, such as training databases, manuals, workbooks, indexed and well-organized documentation, computer-aided instruction, and instructional videos.
- Request cost information on telephone support and follow-up, on-site training.
- Require output measures that insure satisfactory proficiency levels.

Evaluate and analyze vendor responses to training questions as critically as you would the responses to hardware and software specifications. Finalize all aspects of the training program as part of the contract negotiations. This is particularly important in system migrations, when staff is being retrained. Determine when and where training sessions will be held, how many will attend each class, what the level and content of each session will be, and what documentation and training aids—including test databases and audio-visual aids—will be provided.

Remember that resistance to change, unlearning old skills acquired from previous manual or automated systems, and longer learning curves are characteristic of many staff trainees. Do not schedule training sessions too far in advance of when the trainees will actually begin to use the system or subsystem. Make objectives and expectations clear in the beginning, and create a non-threatening training environment.

Particularly when retraining staff, ensure that training sessions are geared to the participants' levels of expertise. For staff already skilled in using an automated system, an emphasis on training in the basic aspects of the system may be unnecessary. Provide an introductory overview of the entire system, and encourage procedural and methodological comparisons with the previous system.

In most instances, systems are sufficiently complex that it will be necessary to have certain staff members receive training in specific components of the system. For each such component, identify a staff member who will work closely with vendor trainers initially and will in turn provide ongoing training for other staff members as required; this person should not be the system administrator. In choosing an in-house training coordinator, enthusiasm and interest should be the primary consideration, rather than just computer expertise.

The training coordinator should:

- assess the knowledge and experience of the vendor trainer(s)
- assess in advance the quality and timeliness of the training aids and documentation, rewriting where necessary
- select an appropriate training area
- select staff to be trained and grouped in classes based on criteria such as level of expertise and curriculum to be covered
- identify trainees with an aptitude to become in-house trainers
- communicate with vendor trainer(s) to discuss the level of training needed for each group and the amount of support that will be provided to subsequent in-house training, including follow-up training

SPECIALIZED STAFF TRAINING

The impact of the Internet and the World Wide Web on automated library systems has resulted in the need to train staff in the development and use of tools needed for the creation of a "virtual" library. The creation and design of Web pages requires significant training in the use of electronic authoring tools and data encoding schemes such as HTML and SGML (respectively, HyperText Markup Language and Standard Generalized Markup Language—see chapter 15). Catalogers must learn to create the MARC field for Electronic Location and Access and link the contents of its subfields, particularly the URL (Uniform Resource Locator), into a Web browser environment for instant user access to the location specified.

Training in these specialized areas may be done in-house but may also require an investment in vendor-run training classes, either on- or off-site. Although training in these areas may seem frivolous, it is becoming ever more necessary for librarians to develop these skills in order to use the array of electronic resources available properly and fully.

TRAINING THE PUBLIC

Public relations is not the first vehicle that comes to mind when we think of training the public, but public acceptance and enthusiasm for your new automated system is an important ingredient in a successful planning effort.

Public relations can accomplish three things:

- It can make users aware of your new system and services.
- It can motivate them to use the system.
- It can train them in using the new system and services effectively.

In developing a training plan, all three of these should be consciously addressed, and each may suggest a different approach. Public training methodologies will vary with the type of library. They may include:

- developing handouts, flyers, and tip sheets geared to the library's clientele
- formal class instruction, particularly in school and academic libraries
- short, focused minicourses on topics such as system overview; searching strategies; understanding a Web browser; developing, using, and removing individual preferences; and customizing searching front ends
- use of volunteers, as well as staff, to provide individualized one-on-one help.

Remember, not all training has to occur in the library. Outreach efforts that take place where users live and work can be just as effective—if not more so—than efforts undertaken on-site. These might include workshops in establishing dial-up connections to your system from home computers.

Whenever possible, try to identify specific user groups for whom customized training can be provided, particularly if training can be tailored to the specific known needs of the group. Such groups might include faculty, friends, community organizations, or groups within your parent organization.

Most systems pride themselves on their intuitive, easy-to-use, public interfaces. As systems move away from textual, menu-driven modules and toward ones functioning in a graphical environment, user training may center more on understanding Windows and using a mouse or trackball than on system functions per se.

CONCLUSION

The following are good guidelines for both staff and public training:

- Involve staff members at all levels in planning activities.
- Evaluate and make effective use of vendor-provided training materials and make sure you receive enough to meet your needs.
- Identify any separate training programs, who will be trained, and individuals who will be responsible for any ongoing training in the area.
- Use training tips to make in-house training effective.

SOURCES

Epple, Margie, et al. "Staff Training and Automated Systems: 20 Tips for Success." *Journal of Academic Librarianship* 18:2 (May 1992), 87–89.

"Training experience within a large academic library system and general training literature provide the basis for this concise guide to developing staff training for automated system use. The guide contains 20 tips that fall into 5 concept areas: trainers; trainees; program content and design; training environment and schedule; and follow-up. The guide may be used for initial system implementation or for subsequent transferals to newer systems."

Freeman, Gretchen L., and Russell Clement. "Critical Issues in Library Automation Staff Training." *Electronic Library* 7:2 (April 1989), 76–82.

This article identifies and discusses issues involved in implementing and maintaining a staff training program, including the use of a phased approach to instruction, the importance of follow-up, and continuity. Contains a useful "New Employee Skills Checklist."

Hallmark, Julie, and C. Rebecca Garcia. "System Migration: Experiences from the Field." *Information Technology and Libraries* 11:4 (December 1992), 345–358.

"Automation administrators of thirty-three libraries discussed challenges, rewards, and problems associated with migration to new automated systems." Among other issues, the interviews dealt with the training of staff and users. "Training for library staff proved to be a problematic part of migration. . . . Aspects of training provided lengthy responses and detailed advice on 'how we would do it differently if we could do it all over again'" (p. 351).

—————————. "Training for Automated Systems in Libraries." *Information Technology and Libraries* 15:3 (September 1996), 157–167.

"In a series of interviews, the automation administrators of forty-nine libraries that had recently installed automated systems discussed staff and user training for their new systems. The interviews focused on training objectives and procedures, timing and effectiveness of the training, and problems encountered. Eight vendors then presented their points of view as they responded to issues raised by librarians."

Litchfield, Charles A. "Vendor Training: A Question of Commitment to User Success." *Journal of Library Administration* 12:2 (1990), 3–12.

"The article explores the role of vendor training in the long-term relationship that exists between libraries that purchase an integrated online library system and vendors that market and support such systems. Emphasis is given to the responsibility vendors have to properly train library personnel so as to insure successful implementation and use of their online system . . ."

Tennant, Roy. "The Virtual Library Foundation: Staff Training and Support." *Information Technology and Libraries* 14:1 (March 1995), 46–49.

"The creation, management, and support of virtual libraries require at all stages skillful and knowledgeable support of library staff." This article focuses on instruction and training methods, varieties of documentation used to support training, and staying up-to-date after training, including remaining aware of what may be possible in the future.

PART III: PLANNING SYSTEM DATABASES

High quality, machine-readable databases are the cornerstone upon which all future automation efforts will rest. Vendors may come and go, hardware may become obsolete, software may be replaced, but well-constructed, well-maintained databases will be the library's transportable and viable links from system to system. A critical part of creating and sustaining high quality databases is adherence to standards, which are covered in detail in chapter 15.

◀1◀1 RETROSPECTIVE CONVERSION

Conversion is the sequence of steps needed to acquire, create, or modify machine-readable records for an automated database. Simply, it is the process whereby records only humans can read are transformed so that computers can read them, too. Converted data may include:

- the card catalog
- the shelflist
- borrower information
- serials check-in records
- citations from indexes
- community information and other referral files
- the text of books and articles
- pictures, illustrations, graphs, and tables.

This chapter looks at the conversion of bibliographic data files, but it is important to keep in mind other types of data as candidates for conversion. These may include textual citation files used for reference and referral, and full-text materials such as reading lists, bibliographies, course syllabi, or catalogs. Image and other graphical files should also be identified and assessed. These types of materials will likely require scanning or direct data entry in order to convert them to machine-readable form. In many cases, their accessibility, once converted, will require a graphical rather than a text-based interface. (Standards used for conversion of non-bibliographic data are discussed in chapter 15.)

Conversion of the card catalog and shelflist is a prerequisite to the effective automation of all traditional library functions. The process is similar in some ways to highway repairs: costly, labor intensive, and aggravating to all those involved. But the result—a high quality, transportable bibliographic database—is worth the temporary inconvenience.

When conversion is undertaken with a library's entire existing collection and current acquisitions, the process is known as *retrospective conversion*. Once you have made the decision to initiate a retrospective conversion project, you must determine the scope of the project by:

- deciding what areas of the collection will be converted
- prioritizing the order in which each area is to be done
- determining the speed with which the conversion must be accomplished.

Write down the scope, goals, and objectives of your project, and be sure everyone involved understands them. Staff participation is very important to the success of any retrospective conversion project. Bring your staff into the planning process from the beginning.

PREPARING FOR CONVERSION

WEEDING AND INVENTORY

Weeding and inventory are crucial precursors to retrospective conversion. Since it costs money to create, process, update, and store each bibliographic record, it is a waste of labor and funds to create records for missing or outdated items.

Weeding can begin now, right this minute. It does not require special funding or budget approvals, but it does require commitment, reallocation of human resources, and adjustments to workflow. On the bright side, weeding will save your library money and time. (A weeding process is described in chapter 12.)

A physical inventory of the collection is important for two reasons: (1) it will prevent conversion of items that have vanished, and (2) it is a critical means of comparing the physical item to its "surrogate," in most cases a shelflist card, so that information, both bibliographic and local holdings, can be matched, corrected, deleted or added. Inventory time is a good time to add unique numeric identifiers such as an LCCN (Library of Congress *Card* Number—not to be confused with the LC *class* number) and an ISBN (International Standard Book Number) or ISSN (International Standard Serial Number) to the shelflist, if they do not already appear. These numbers should be obtained only from the item itself or from a MARC record (MARC—MAchine Readable Cataloging—standards are discussed later). *Books in Print* should not be used as a source for these numbers because the numbers sometimes change. When feasible, both an LCCN and an ISBN should be added to monographs and an LCCN and ISSN to serials. Be wary of using LCCNs printed in paperbacks; they are often for the hardback edition.

Here are examples of the numeric identifiers mentioned above.
LCCN: 65-9908
LC Class Number: Z 1011 .B63 1990
ISBN: 0-8103-0586-0
ISSN: 0524-0581

FILE IDENTIFICATION

It is also important to analyze—to identify, describe, and document—all of the library's manual files that are to be converted. A method for analyzing the shelflist file is presented further on, but don't forget all those other files that lurk in your library, such as:

- serials check-in files
- order files
- borrower files
- overdues
- product files
- clipping files
- resource files for community information or other special purposes.

Without this analysis, it is difficult to determine the costs that will be required not only for a retrospective conversion but also for the automated system itself. You should obtain the following information from this effort:

- how the file is used
- number of records in the file
- types of information contained in each record (e.g., for an overdue: title, call number, date due, borrower name, amount of fine; for a serials check-in: title, volume number, issue/part number, date received)
- number of records added, deleted, or changed daily, weekly, monthly, and annually
- methods of file maintenance
- frequency of file use
- extent and type of duplication of information in other files
- how well data elements conform to specific standards (see chapter 15) and the types of variations that are present.

Start looking at your files early on. It is not necessary to examine a file in its entirety. Usually, a sampling is sufficient for collecting the information required for analysis. (For the shelflist, this should be done *after* the completion of a weeding/inventory program, so that missing and discarded titles do not affect the final result.) Analysis of the sample provides the information required to implement the most cost-effective and efficient data conversion method or methods. Different sampling techniques exist for providing a valid sample from which to draw the information that you need (see list of sources for further reading), or you may choose to devise one of your own.

METHODS AND COSTS

STEPS IN THE CONVERSION PROCESS

It may be useful at this point to briefly outline the actual steps involved in a typical conversion project:

Step 1: Using the information from the library's existing catalog (usually the shelflist), the library or a contract service vendor locates matching computerized bibliographic records, generally through a computer search of the MARC database first and other resource databases subsequently.

Step 2: Matching bibliographic records are verified as correct matches, are edited to conform to the cataloging practices of the library doing the converting, are extracted from the resource databases, and are then added to a separate machine-readable collection database for that library.

Step 3: The library (or contractor) then creates machine-readable records for titles in the library's collection *not* located in any of the resource databases. This record is most commonly a full bibliographic record (containing all the information on the 3x5 catalog card), but may be only a short entry.

Step 4: The library's new bibliographic database can now be used as the basis for a computerized online catalog, circulation system, or other automated system.

DATA CONVERSION METHODS

Data conversion methods most commonly used are:

- in-house conversion, using existing staff
- outsourced in-house conversion, using outside contract labor
- outsourced off-site conversion, with a service vendor doing the keying.

There are advantages and disadvantages to each of the above methods.

In-house conversions using existing staff
- incur lower up-front per item costs
- allow files to remain on-site.

However, hidden costs such as:

- impact on existing workflow
- excessively long timelines for project completion
- additional space and hardware requirements
- added supervisory and quality control efforts
- increased personnel costs

may in fact make in-house conversions more costly in the long run.

Outsourced in-house conversions using outside contract labor
- allow files to remain in the library
- lessen the negative impact on work flow and staff time.

However:

- Space must be found for the additional temporary personnel
- There must be access to a database against which to match and convert your records (as with any in-house conversion).

This database may be an online bibliographic utility such as OCLC, a MARC file on compact disk, or a PC-based batch conversion system. Thus:

- There may be competition for the same equipment, requiring the introduction of multiple shifts.

Outsourced, off-site vendor-keyed conversion
In this, each item in the collection—as described in the shelflist—is matched to a database owned by the vendor. This means that:

- Conversion will cost more per item
- Shelflists will probably have to leave the library.

Photocopying is possible but:

- is extremely labor-intensive
- will incur additional costs for supplies.

NOTE

As stated earlier, most libraries convert their collections from their *shelflists*. Shelflist cards are the most efficient conversion medium, since they bibliographically mirror the item (presumably) and are compact and easily transportable. *Accession books* generally do not provide sufficient information. *Public catalogs* are usable, but include multiple cards for each item, posing a redundancy problem. Conversion can be done from the *item itself*, but this is cumbersome and requires the removal and replacement of each item.

Accession books, public catalogs, and physical items do not lend themselves to off-site conversions. Therefore, if off-site conversion is the method selected, it may be necessary to create shelflist cards either for those items without them or if the library lacks a shelflist file altogether.

Performance measures and quality control concerns must be contractually negotiated, since there will be little direct control by the library over these. However, contracting with an outside vendor will result in predefined costs and time frames for completion. A vendor-keyed conversion can therefore often be performed more efficiently with much less impact on a library's day-to-day operations.

In practice, a hybrid approach is often adopted in which all three methods are used. The bulk of the monograph collection may be sent to a vendor to be converted off-site, while more difficult materials such as serials, nonprint, and local history may be converted on-site using either existing staff or contract labor.

RETROSPECTIVE CONVERSION COSTS

The cost of a vendor-keyed conversion can range from approximately $0.60 to $2.00 per record and includes creation of the bibliographic database, creation of item-level holdings fields, and application of authority control. The average cost, if the high end of the range is eliminated, is approximately $0.90 per record.

Factors affecting cost include:

- the size of the collection
- the publication dates and languages of included items
- the fullness of records being provided
- how closely local cataloging matches national standards.

Special formats such as serials and nonprint materials are more difficult to convert than monographs. Videos, foreign language materials, and older local history and genealogical titles that must be originally cataloged may cost as much as $20.00 per record. A collection sampling will provide the data needed to determine these factors and their cost implications.

The cost elements of an in-house conversion should include the cost of a database against which to convert. The most expensive options are the online bibliographic utilities such as OCLC, WLN, and Brodart. The least expensive are the batch conversion systems consisting of software packages that run on personal computers. LCCN or ISBN numbers are keyed in, and the data is either electronically transmitted or saved on diskettes and sent to the vendor supplying the program. The library's database is created by matching the numbers to the bibliographic records in the vendor's database.

The MARC files are also available through the World Wide Web or on CD-ROM from a number of vendors. This is a mid-priced option that allows the library offline, in-house access to full bibliographic records. Other costs associated with in-house conversions are equipment purchase or rental, space allocation, and personnel.

DOING A SHELFLIST ANALYSIS

Identifying, describing, and documenting existing shelflist files and the data they contain is an important preconversion activity. It enables you to determine variations in catalog card entries that can lead to inconsistencies and errors in your new machine-readable record. It also makes it possible for you to discover past and current cataloging practices that may result in a "no-match" or mismatch during retrospective conversion.

You can perform a shelflist analysis either by using a sampling method or simply by browsing through the cards in your shelflist. (For different methods, see the sources listed at the end of the chapter.) The analysis will field data for a *holdings matrix*, which will allow you to standardize entries and will serve as a guide for your ongoing cataloging efforts.

Certain areas in the collection tend to contain a high degree of catalog variation, so it probably is a good idea to start by examining the shelflist cards for these areas:

- reference
- audio-visual and any other nonprint material
- local history
- foreign language
- 910 to 920 in the Dewey call number sequence for nonfiction (the problem here is with serials that are cataloged as monographs, such as certain travel guides; in the Library of Congress system, these are found in the E and F classes).

WHAT TO LOOK FOR

A number of cataloging practices can affect the accuracy of any potential retrospective conversion by causing a no-match or an incorrect match. These practices may be grouped into five major areas:

1. *Collection designators* (e.g., "Ref," "Juv," or "Young Adult," call numbers, and main entry cutters) are often not standardized, are inconsistently placed or used, are missing, or are simply incorrect.
2. *Serials* are often cataloged as monographs, are missing volume and/or part information, or are not recataloged and given separate bibliographic records when their titles change.
3. *Multiple editions* are listed on a shelflist that describes *one* edition only.
4. *Missing matching points* occur when shelflist records contain so little bibliographic information that it would be impossible to create a record for them.
5. *Miscellaneous problems:* Shelflist records are missing, illegible, misfiled, represent items that no longer exist, belong to other libraries, are ephemeral (i.e., not destined for conversion), or contain possibly incomplete or inaccurate information provided by the vendors from whom libraries receive their materials preprocessed.

A checklist of other common problems can be found in Figure 11–1.

CREATING A HOLDINGS MATRIX

Once the shelflist has been analyzed and the problems noted, the next step is to create a holdings list that links various pieces of

Figure 11–1 Checklist of Shelflist Problems: A Sampling

1. The shelflist contains so little bibliographic information that it will be impossible to create a record for the item.
2. There are inconsistencies in the creation of call numbers for some types of material.
3. There is little consistency or standardization in the placement of call number information on the card.
4. Title page as opposed to predominant form cataloging is employed inconsistently for assignment of main entry.
5. Successive title cataloging for serials has not been followed, resulting in titles being changed on existing shelflists instead of being created as a new bibliographic record.
6. Title main entries have been incorrectly replaced with personal authors.
7. Author and main entry cutters sometimes appear and sometimes do not. The number of letters in the cutter varies.
8. Titles have been changed on shelflists, but other information such as collation and imprint have been left unchanged.
9. New shelflists have not been created for different editions of a work, with the result that items are listed incorrectly on a given shelflist.
10. For titles in paperback, shelflists must reflect the bibliographic information for the paperback, not the hardcover edition.
11. Publication dates have been altered on shelflists without other data elements being edited.
12. Volume and part information is not indicated on the shelflist. (This is especially crucial for open entries.)
13. Many of the AV items and sound recordings are lacking producer names and/or numbers.
14. Federal documents have no shelflists and are inventoried via an accession book methodology.
15. Serials have been cataloged as monographs.
16. Pagination, LCCN, and ISBN/ISSN are missing.
17. Different editions of the same work are entered on the same shelflist.
18. Multiple copies of the same edition of a work are on different shelflists (e.g., a given copy of a title is listed on both the circulating and reference shelflist with an "also in" note).
19. Shelflists in a given section lack that section's designator on them or else contain differing abbreviations in various locations (e.g., a local history section without a designator).
20. Not all foreign language materials have the language stamped or written on the shelflist.
21. Mysteries and oversized materials are shelved separately, but this is not indicated on the shelflist.
22. Many shelflist cards have been misfiled.
23. Many shelflist cards are illegible.

24. There are shelflist cards filed for items belonging to a different library.
25. Shelflists for ephemeral materials that will remain uncataloged have not been removed.
26. Information on preprocessed shelflists, such as those from Baker & Taylor and Brodart, has not been verified.
27. Nonvalidated subject headings have been assigned. (This is not critical as long as LC subject headings are accepted as they appear in the conversion records.)
28. Author cutters sometimes appear and sometimes do not. The number of letters in the cutter varies. (A consistent cuttering methodology should be decided upon and implemented, and any retrospective conversion vendor should be instructed to follow that methodology regardless of what appears on the shelflist.)
29. Many serial shelflists have latest and earlier edition notes, which may be difficult to reconcile with specific copy information.
30. Many juvenile shelflists include reading levels as part of the call number. (This information should be in a note field, and vendors should be instructed not to include it in the call number field.)
31. Open entries tend to have individual holding years written in pencil to the right of the main entry.
32. A true union shelflist does not exist for the main building and the branches.
33. Shelflists for collections that no longer exist are still in the file. (They should be removed.)
34. Designators on the shelflist are not changed as items are moved in and out of certain collections.

Note: Those responsible for retrospective conversion should be told to ignore elements on the shelflists that have nothing to do with conversion—e.g., multicolored dots, old numbers.

information into a matrix-like representation of the library's collection. This list should be composed of as many of the following elements as are applicable:

- *Library name:* A separate listing should be created for each branch site or separate physical facility.
- *Material type*: e.g., book, paperback, sound recording, film.
- *Collection indicator*: the category of material represented by the designators on the shelflist card (e.g., JUV, REF, YA).
- *Location:* where items are situated in the library (e.g., juvenile stacks, reference office, music room).
- *Shelflist variants:* the different designators used in the shelflist to identify a particular part of the collection.
- *Circulation category:* usually either reference or circulating.

The purpose of this list is to act as a guide in conjunction with current cataloging to assure consistency in cataloging practices, and to standardize input in the creation of local holdings fields, and to be a locating device for information on the shelflist.

Once the matrix has been created, it is important to maintain it, so that it reflects any changes in cataloging practice. New materials, such as videocassettes or computer software, should have parameters established and be added to the matrix when they are added to the collection.

An example of a holdings matrix is shown in Figure 11–2.

SOURCES

Duval, Beverly K. *Automated Library Systems: A Librarian's Guide and Teaching Manual.* Westport, CT: Meckler, 1992.

Chapter 5, entitled "Retrospective Conversion" (pp. 99–132), explains MARC, MicroLIF, the relationship between automating and doing a retrospective conversion, benefits and problems, steps in the planning process, options for conversion, vendor procedures, and costs.

"Retrospective Conversion: Issues and Perspectives; a forum edited by Jon Drabenstott." *Library Hi Tech* 4:2 (Issue 14, Summer 1986), 105–120.

Six consultants present their thinking on some of the basic conversion issues and options and explore why retrospective conversion can be so "troublesome" to librarians.

Schottlaender, Brian, ed. "Retrospective Conversion: History, Approaches, Considerations." *Cataloging and Classification Quarterly* 14:3/4, 1992. *(Issue also published as a monograph by Haworth Press [New York], 1992.)*

Three especially noteworthy articles from this issue are:

Bolin, Mary K., and Harley B. Wright. "Retrospective Conversion of a Medium-Sized Academic Library," pp. 35–50. "This article describes methods the library used to convert its collections, and examines the problems encountered with each method."

Lentz, Edward Adrian. "Editing Recon Records: When Is Enough, Enough? A Selective Review of the Literature," pp. 129–144. Reviews issues of quality control, costs, special material formats, and collections related to editing records retrieved by bibliographic utilities.

Maccaferri, James Tilio. "Managing Authority Control in a Retrospective Conversion Project," pp. 145–167. Considers the objectives of authority control, the degree it is needed in a recon process, and options available to implement authority control in this context.

Figure 11–2 Sample Holdings List

Branch	Media	Collection Indicator	Location	Shelflist Variants	Circulation Category
Name	1. Book 2. Paperback Book	New Jersey	Ref	1. NJ Coll B Subject's last name 2. NJ coll Call # 3. NJ coll J call #	Ref
Name	1. Book 2. Paperback Book	Office	Front Desk	1. Office 2. Office call # 3. REF office 4. Office REF call #	Ref
Name	AV	Office	Front Desk	1. Office slides booklet 2. Office slides cassette	Circ
Name	1. Book 2. Paperback Book	Young Adult Fiction	1. Juv Stacks 2. Juv New Book	1. YA Author's last name 2. YA 1st 3 letters author's last name	Circ
Name	1. Book 2. Paperback Book	Young Adult Biography	1. Juv Stacks 2. Juv New Book	1. YAB Subject's last name 2. YA B Subject's last name	Circ
Name	AV	Game	Front Desk	Game	Circ

12 MAINTAINING THE BIBLIOGRAPHIC DATABASE

The library's bibliographic database created through a retrospective conversion will not be a static one. Titles will be added, withdrawn, transferred, and recataloged. Therefore, plans must be made for ongoing "maintenance" of the database, which can be done through your integrated, online system—assuming that the library is not a member of OCLC or some other bibliographic utility. This is why the cataloging subsystem is so important, for it is through this subsystem that you will be able to create, add, display, edit, delete, replace, and move bibliographic as well as item records in your database.

However, there may be an interim period between when you create your machine-readable database and when your online system is up and running. If your database is not effectively maintained during this interim, bibliographic information will become inaccurate as materials are added and deleted from your collection. Moreover, much of the value of converting holdings information as part of the retrospective conversion process may be lost, since any changes made subsequent to the conversion will not be captured.

MAINTENANCE OPTIONS

If a lengthy interim period is projected, your library may wish to wait to convert its local holdings information, keep paper records of title deletions and changes, and outsource the ongoing conversion of new titles. Or it may explore methodologies for loading, using, and maintaining your database online until an integrated system has been selected and implemented.

The ongoing conversion of new titles can be accomplished in a variety of ways, including:

- Catalog or contract to have materials cataloged on a bibliographic utility such as OCLC or Brodart or by another library or network of libraries in your area

- Obtain MARC records from companies, such as Marcive, that specialize in providing such services to libraries
- Use systems such as Bibliofile (Library Corporation) or SuperCat (Gaylord) that provide access to the MARC files on CD-ROM (compact disc) for local creation of new title records.

NOTE

A contractual arrangement for maintenance can be agreed to either as part of the retrospective conversion contract or separately. The costs associated with retrospective conversion may become more competitive if a vendor anticipates ongoing activity with the database. This does not preclude, however, choosing one vendor for retrospective conversion and another for ongoing maintenance.

If your database is to be maintained at a remote location, the tapes created by the retrospective conversion will be sent to the vendor with whom your library has outsourced the maintenance of its database. You should forward to the vendor all additions, deletions, and changes as they occur in your collection so that the database would be continually updated and kept current.

You may wish to have local access to your database, however, in order to make it available for a service-related function such as a public access catalog. Here, your database can be maintained in such a way that you have regular, direct access to it in one of two ways:

- A vendor hosts the database and provides you with telephone line or Internet access to it.
- The database is "mastered" onto disks or CD-ROMs that are accessed through a workstation or a LAN actually situated in your library. (These databases may be used later on as a back-up to the online, interactive catalog.)

Additions, changes, and deletions to the database would then be handled in a variety of ways:

- Your library would directly maintain (modify) its existing holdings—by telephone, over the Internet, or locally through vendor-supplied software.
- New titles would be converted using one of the methods described previously.

COST FACTORS

The costs of maintaining your database after retrospective conversion depend on the mix of maintenance options you choose. If your database, or any part of it, is maintained at a remote location, you incur charges for the cataloging of new titles, for deletions and changes, and for the storage of your database in a computer. If you maintain your existing holdings yourself, you pay either for telephone line and/or Internet connection charges to access the database remotely (in addition to online storage charges), or for vendor-supplied software to access the database locally (in your library).

Using your database as an offline public catalog will mean incurring additional costs, such as:

- a database set-up charge
- per title charges for mastering and producing the database
- the cost of purchasing public catalog workstations
- the cost of the public catalog software
- the cost of compact disks for a CD-ROM catalog.

Keeping your new machine-readable bibliographic database accurate and up-to-date is an essential part of automation planning and crucial to the success of your automation efforts. The system you install is only as usable as the database that supports it.

WEEDING

Materials are weeded from the library in order to maintain a current, active, and useful collection. Weeding should always be part of a library's ongoing program of collection assessment and development.

The weeding process described in this section is based on objective criteria that are simple and straightforward. But weeding involves both objective and subjective judgment: objective criteria can provide guidelines, but they cannot replace professional decision making.

METHODOLOGY

Begin by establishing a timeline by which the weeding of different parts of the collection needs to be completed. If you take small, defined steps, the process will seem less overwhelming. For example, you might decide that adult and juvenile fiction will be weeded by (choose a date), and adult and juvenile nonfiction will be weeded by (choose a date). At the point that you become convinced that weeding is actually doable, set deadlines for the rest of your collection. And remember, there are no sacred cows when it comes to weeding.

WEEDING FORM

Staff (check)
_____Usage
_____Duplicate
_____Superseded
_____Condition

Librarian (check)
_____Withdraw
_____Return to shelf
_____Repair/bindery

If your library is at one site, complete weeding for the entire library. If the library has a branch or two, complete it for one site. Here are the steps to follow in the weeding process:

1. *Assign staff* to identify books that are eligible for weeding on the basis of any of the following criteria:

   - books published, for example, in 1980 or earlier that have not circulated in the last five years
   - books that are *exact* duplicates of another book
   - books that are earlier editions superseded by a later edition that is on the shelf
   - books that are in poor physical condition.

2. *Exceptions* to the areas to be weeded include the following:

   - all literature and literary criticism
   - all local history and archival material
   - special collections established in commemoration of a local person or event
   - anything written by a local author.

3. *Procedures* for weeding:
   - Take a book truck, check-off pads (see sample form at left), and pencil (or pen) to stack section to be weeded.
   - Begin to scan shelves, in order, for candidates to be weeded.
   - Examine books, applying criteria for weeding.
   - When a book meets any of the criteria for weeding, remove the book to the book truck and check off the reason(s) for removal on a pad slip. Place the slip in the book.
   - When finished with a section, bring books to be considered for weeding to where a librarian may review them.
   - The librarian will make the final decision and indicate it on the slip.
   - Books will be moved to appropriate areas of the library according to the librarian's decision.

(Suggestion: Locate and prepare adequate storage space to hold the books removed from the shelves.)

4. *Return a book to the shelf* if there is any doubt about the wisdom of withdrawing the book, based upon:
   - known in-house use patterns (e.g., sources used routinely in the library but that never circulate)
   - inherent importance of the title (e.g., if the book is a classic)
   - necessary duplication (e.g., multiple copies of bestsellers or titles on reading lists)
   - need to retain superseded edition because of its special value (e.g., unique illustrations or a special introduction by a renowned authority in the earlier, original edition)
   - other factors.

A book should also be returned to the shelf if, based on further inspection, it can be repaired or rebound instead of being weeded.

5. *Keep accurate statistics* on the number of items actually withdrawn from the collection.

SOURCE

Slote, Stanley J. *Weeding Library Collections: Library Weeding Methods*. 4th ed. Englewood, CO: Libraries Unlimited, forthcoming.

First published in 1975, the 3d edition (1989) is still available. The author shows how to identify the core collections versus the weedable collections and discusses a variety of traditional and computer-assisted methods for weeding. This is a practical guide that outlines step-by-step procedures.

13 BAR CODING

Almost everyone is familiar with the zebra-striped labels that have become ubiquitous in our lives, from the supermarket line to the materials that we buy for our libraries. Bar codes owe their success to the design that allows unique information to be programmed into their stripes and then read accurately and quickly by readers and scanners attached to computers.

Bar codes have become an indispensable part of library automation because they serve as a computerized accession number—a unique identifier that links a specific book, journal, compact disk, and the like—to the computerized bibliographic record that describes it.

WHAT IS IT?

Bar coding attaches a bar code label to an item in the library's collection or to a borrower's library card. There are several ways to bar code the items associated with your materials files, borrower files, and other files that you must link to the correct electronic records in your bibliographic, borrower, and other appropriate databases.

SMART BAR CODES

One popular method for labeling and linking the collection utilizes customized, or smart, bar codes. Smart bar codes are created by means of computerized processing of the item information already contained in the bibliographic record. The item information is then linked to a unique number and a corresponding bar code label is printed that, as suggested below, includes a mix of eye-readable matching points such as call number, location, truncated author and/or title, publication date, and edition.

YOUR LIBRARY NAME (35)
CALL NUMBER (40)   **Location (9)**
Title of this book (40 positions)
Author's Name (40)

3 1234 56789004 9

You should consider this method if your collection has already been retrospectively converted and contains the information necessary to create the item record through machine processing. It will be most successful if item information has been entered consistently, if call numbers are unique, and if database maintenance is up-to-date so that bar codes are not created for items that, for example, have been withdrawn from the collection. Libraries using the Dewey Decimal Classification can still use smart bar codes as long as enough eye-readable information is printed on the bar code label to identify the item clearly.

Smart bar codes cost more than generic bar codes initially both for production of the labels and for the machine processing required to support their use. Common problems in smart bar coding projects include:

- items for which no label has been printed—principally duplicate copies, multivolume sets, and items for which there was no information in the database
- creating bar code labels for nonexistent items
- creating bar codes with insufficient identifying information to match them with the item on the shelf.

Because a smart bar code has already been attached to an item in the automated system, any human error that results in attaching the wrong bar code to the wrong item will have very negative implications.

Smart bar codes do have advantages, however:

- Materials do not have to be physically transported to workstations to be linked.
- The bar coding and linking process can be completed in one step, saving personnel costs.
- There is little "on-the-fly" conversion to deal with at the circulation desk.

It is less important to attach an eye-readable bar code number to the shelflist, particularly if the shelflist is to be closed following the completion of the automation project. However, if the shelflist is being maintained, it is helpful to attach a label that is both eye- and machine-readable.

GENERIC BAR CODES

For those libraries that have not completed retrospective conversion or that do not have sufficient item information in their bibliographic records to make the use of smart bar codes practical, the use of generic, or "dumb," bar codes may be the best approach. Dumb bar codes have no inherent connection to an item and basically consist of a bar code and an eye-readable number that can be attached randomly to materials in the collection. The sample below is printed courtesy of the Bergen County Cooperative Library System (BCCLS) of Hackensack, NJ.

3 9198 05003641 4

There are two ways to utilize dumb bar codes:

1. Take the items to be bar coded and linked to a terminal, bar code each item, then link the item into the system by matching it with the appropriate bibliographic record, transferring necessary item information, and wanding, scanning or keying the bar code number to complete the process. (Note: It is often useful to have the shelflist available, since all of the necessary information may not be available or readily visible on the piece itself.)
2. Take the shelflist to the shelves, bar code both the item and the shelflist, then link the item into the system from the shelflist.

Items can also be linked "on-the-fly" at the circulation desk using dumb bar codes.

The disadvantages to this method are apparent. Either all items in the collection must be moved to and from workstations, or a two-step process of labeling and linking must be adopted, which takes longer and requires more human labor.

However, dumb bar codes are less expensive than smart bar codes, and there are no machine processing costs incurred. It is also less likely that items will be mislinked, since the bar codes have not been preassigned to a specific bibliographic record.

Some prefer on-the-fly conversion since only those items in the collection that are being used are initially bar coded. However, this method can cause congestion at the circulation desk and, with the proliferation of online catalogs, can prevent items from being used simply because they have not been linked and are therefore not accessible through the OPAC.

Often combining both dumb and smart bar codes results in the most successful projects. Smart bar codes can be used most effectively with monographs, while serials, continuations, and multivolume sets are better labeled and linked using dumb bar codes.

Dumb bar codes are generally used for linking borrowers to a database because preloading of borrower information is not as widespread as preloading of item information. In some cases, registration or personnel tapes may be available so that borrower information can also be processed using smart bar codes.

HOW TO GET BAR CODES

Bar codes may be purchased as singles (1 zebra stripe/eye-readable label), doubles (1 zebra stripe and 2 eye-readable labels), duplicates (2 zebra stripes/eye-readable labels), or triplicates (3 zebra stripes/eye-readable labels). When using dumb bar codes, it is wise to put at least an eye-readable bar code number on the shelflist and borrower registration forms during an initial conversion. Later, if paper files are dispensed with, a single combination bar code and eye-readable number can be used.

There are several bar code formats available. The ones most used by library automation systems have fourteen-digit numbers using either the Codabar or Code 39, also known as Code 3 of 9, designs. These bar code labels have the following structure:

Digit:	1	2 3 4 5	6 7 8 9 10 11 12 13	14
Meaning:	Item Type	Institution Number	Item or Patron Identification Number	Check Digit

This structure may be described further as follows:

ITEM TYPE: Distinguishes materials from patrons.

INSTITUTION NUMBER: A four-digit number representing the library (institution) whose bar code this is. Use either your institution's OCLC Name Address Control Number (NACN) or obtain a number from the bar code registry maintained by GEAC Computers, Inc. by calling 1-800-825-2574 and asking for Inside Sales. GEAC provides bar code registry as a free service without obligation.

ITEM OR PATRON IDENTIFICATION NUMBER: This is a sequentially-assigned, eight-digit number representing the items in a library's collection. Begin numbering with 00000001.

CHECK DIGIT: This is a modulus-10, type-1 check digit, which is calculated using the values of digits 1-13.

BAR CODING BEFORE BUYING A SYSTEM

It is possible to bar code a collection prior to selecting a system, and can be particularly efficient to do so during an inventory process. If you choose to do this, remember that:

- You must choose one of the two standard formats.
- You need to include the standard number of digits, including a check digit.
- Item labels must be numerically distinguishable from borrower labels.

If you go this route, you must attend scrupulously to database maintenance during the interim period. This can be very time-consuming and difficult if the database cannot be easily accessed. Dumb bar codes are probably the better choice in cases such as this, particularly if the lag time between labeling and system implementation will be more than just a few months. Regardless of the type of bar code chosen, it is highly desirable to attach a bar code to the shelflist if labeling is done prior to system selection.

It is advisable, for purposes of durability, to purchase labels with a laminate coating, although these are slightly more expensive. It is also important to include the name of the library on the label bearing the zebra stripe coding along with the eye-readable identifier, as shown in the examples.

Before beginning to bar code, you must decide where on the item the bar code will be placed. There are several possibilities. One is to put the bar code in the upper left hand corner of the outside front cover of a book. This allows easy accessibility during charge-out and check-in and, for inventory purposes, allows the label to be seen easily when the item is on the shelf. Labels may be placed vertically or horizontally, with the position determined by what the staff considers to be easiest to wand and scan.

If duplicate or triplicate bar codes are used, one can be placed on the outside of the book and another in a more protected location inside the item. The costs associated with duplicate and triplicate labels, however, are significantly higher than those for single or double labels.

The bar code can also be placed inside the book near the book pocket, particularly if the book must be opened anyway to insert a date due card.

Libraries with round-the-clock access, but lacking round-the-clock staffing, may wish to place one bar code label on the book and one on the book card itself, so that books can be charged easily when staff returns. Libraries located in hospitals and corporations may fall into this category.

Finally, labeling more exotic items such as compact disks, filmstrips, toys, and equipment require more creative placement schemes. Often in these cases, the labels end up on the packaging, rather than on the piece itself.

THE BAR CODING PROJECT

Placing bar codes on materials can be done in-house by staff and/or volunteers, or the project may be outsourced. If multiple bar codes are being placed on materials, shelflists, and/or book cards, working in teams of two helps ensure that duplicate or triplicate pairs are not mismatched. Written instructions (see Figure 13–1) make the project easier for everyone, especially if you use volunteers or contract labor.

SOURCES

Buschman, John, et al. "Smart Barcoding in a Small Academic Library." *Information Technology and Libraries* 7:3 (September 1988), 263–270.

"This article describes the smart barcoding of the circulating collection in a small university library with limited funds and personnel. . . . Specific details of methodology are . . . incorporated so that the article may guide other libraries with restricted resources."

Epstein, Susan Baerg, et al. "Custom Barcoding as a Better Way." *Library Journal*, 114:14 (September 1, 1989), 156–159.

Describes the use of and rationale behind custom (smart) bar code labels. Planning and preparation are emphasized. The article discusses whether or not to close the library, and dealing with problems and discrepancies that arise. It presents recommendations that are especially useful for library systems with many variously-sized branch locations.

Figure 13-1 Instructions for a Bar Coding Project

WHAT TEAMS OF TWO PEOPLE WILL NEED
- Book truck
- Pencils
- Scrap cards
- Shelflist drawer
- Sheets of item bar code labels

PLACEMENT OF BAR CODES ON SHELFLIST CARDS
1. Get a shelflist drawer.
2. Put a 3x5 card with the team names in the front of the drawer, leaving room for more writing on the card. If there is already a card, start where the last team finished.
3. Remove the rod from the shelflist drawer.
4. Go to the shelf position for the first item in the shelflist drawer, or to the place where the last work was done on the project. You will work from the shelf to the shelflist drawer.
5. One person will read aloud from the spine the call number and title of an item. The second person will locate the shelflist card and bar code labels. Note: Smart bar code labels will have call numbers and titles printed on the labels.
6. The bar code labels come in matched pairs. Be certain that you are using the *matched pair*.
7. When you have a matching physical item and shelflist card, attach a bar code label to the physical item.
8. Put the companion bar code label on the back of the shelflist card. Note: If there is a third label, it may be put inside the item or on the book card.
9. For multivolume/copy books:
    a. Put the bar code on the shelflist, making sure the volume-identifying information is clearly matched to the bar code number.
    b. Make new bar code cards if all of the volumes/copies will not fit on the existing shelflist cards.
    c. When you must start new cards for serials or items with multiple volumes, use a *blank* card with the following information:
        i. format (if other than book)
        ii. call number
        iii. title; after the title, put "bar code card #2," or whatever card number this will be.
    d. Begin placing the bar codes in a column starting in the lower left-hand corner of the shelflist and continuing up the side. Begin the second column at the bottom of the shelflist. Leave space at the side for volume or year information.

>   e. Because of their width, do not put more than two columns of bar codes on a card.
>   f. Put bar codes on both sides of the card.
>   g. When all volumes are done, you may staple the shelflist cards together, if practical.
> 10. Return the shelflist card to the drawer and the item to the shelf.
> 11. Continue to the next item on the shelf.
> 12. Stand up any shelflists for which there is no item on the shelf.
> 13. If you stop work before you finish a drawer, note on the 3x5 card in the front of the drawer where you left off and the date.
> 14. When a drawer is completed, write "bar coded," the date completed, and the team members' names on the 3x5 card.
>
> **PLACEMENT OF BAR CODES ON PACKAGING MATERIALS**
> 15. Attach the bar code label, when possible, to the outside upper left-hand corner of the front cover of items.
> 16. Try not to cover information that may be on the cover of the item.
> 17. If there is a very loose transparent cover on the item, put the bar code *under* the plastic, directly on the item. If there is no room to put the bar code under the plastic, put it *on* the plastic.
> 18. Press the labels firmly to be sure they will stick.
> 19. On compact disk cases: Put the bar code label in the upper right-hand corner.
> 20. On other nonprint materials (e.g., slides, filmstrips)
>   a. Determine the upper left-hand corner of most boxes by positioning the box so that the edge title label is read as a book spine, with the box standing on its bottom edge, the top opening to the right.
>   b. With boxes that have removable (not hinged) bottoms (usually filmstrips and slides), put the bar code labels on the lid.

> **CHECK-OFF FORM FOR BAR CODING PROBLEMS**
>
> TITLE:
>
> ____ Item has no shelflist card
> ____ Shelflist card is misfiled
> ____ Other:

Gatten, Jeffrey N. "Bar Coding Projects: Preparation and Execution." *Library Hi Tech* 8:1 (Issue 29, 1990), 21–27.

"This article attempts to provide a comprehensive overview of the relevant issues for a successful bar coding project. Selecting bar codes, planning and structuring a project, calculating time estimates and maintaining staff morale are presented in detail. A selected bibliography provides access to more information."

14 MACHINE-READABLE CATALOGING

If you are going to automate your library, then paper files (such as the card catalog), the shelflist, authority files, and community information referral files must be in a form that a computer can read. When these files are laid out in a *standardized* manner, they become machine readable—i.e., comprehensible to a computer.

MARC, short for MAchine Readable Cataloging, constitutes a group of communications formats that conforms to the American National Standard for Bibliographic Information Interchange (NISO Z39.2). It is the vehicle for converting bibliographic paper files to machine-readable ones.

MARC

MARC was originally developed by the Library of Congress in the 1960s as a means of translating the information on catalog cards into a format that could be read, stored, and processed by a computer. Initially known as the "LC MARC" format, it is now referred to as USMARC, although the two terms are still often used interchangeably.

In the MARC format, each discrete title, often equivalent to a shelflist card, becomes a bibliographic record. Similarly, each card in an authority file, including the cross-reference cards in the catalog, becomes an authority record. Cards in referral files become community information records.

Here are some basics about the layout of a MARC record:

- *Fields:* Each item of information—personal, corporate or meeting name, title, imprint, facility, program, subject, and so on—is assigned its own special place, called a field within the MARC record. Each field must have an address or label that tells the computer what kind of information the field contains. Using full words like "title" and "subject" takes up too much storage space within the computer, so three-digit numbers called *tags* replace these descriptive terms. Using digits also guarantees that fields are called the same thing every time.

For example:
– 245 tag marks the title information field
– 100 tag marks the personal name field
– 856 tag marks the electronic location and access field

- *Subfields:* Sometimes the information within a field must be broken down further. For example, the "electronic location and access" field includes the name of the electronic host, its location, and the Uniform Resource Locator (URL) World Wide Web address. Each piece of information must be preceded by the equivalent of an apartment number in order for the (dumb) computer to understand where one ends and another begins.

  To conserve space, the descriptive terms are replaced by a single lower-case letter called *subfield codes*, which are preceded by a special character called a *subfield delimiter* (≠). Because many keyboards cannot create the delimiter, other special characters, such as an underline (_) or a dollar sign ($) may be used. The subfield codes are standardized so that the same ones always appear to define a specific piece of information within a given field.

  Field tags may also be followed by one or two single-digit *indicators*, which represent values that interpret or supplement the data found in the field. Each indicator has its own discrete meaning. In the following example, the "1" represents the need for a separate title entry in the catalog and the "4" represents the number of nonfiling characters at the beginning of the field:

  24514$a The American heritage guide to antiques /$cMary Durant.

  Tags, subfield codes, and indicators together are referred to as *content designators*. They describe the contents of the fields in terms that a computer can understand. Records that include these content designators are referred to as *tagged records*.

- Each tagged record also has a *leader* and a *directory*. The leader is the first twenty-four characters of the record and contains programming information for the computer. The directory tells what tags are in the record and describes their placement. The directory is necessary because the MARC Communications Format formats the record into a long continuous string of fields with no tags. The directory explains to the computer how to reformat the record, after its transfer, into usable fields of data.

- The last important segment of a MARC bibliographic record is the *008 field*, Fixed-Length Data Elements, also known as "Fixed Field Codes." It provides such information as whether the item being described in the record is a monograph or serial, what country it was published in, the subject heading system for an authority record, facilities availability for a community information record, and its frequency (if it is a serial).

WHY IS MARC SO IMPORTANT?

The most time-consuming and perhaps most expensive activity that you will undertake to automate your library is converting your manual files to machine-readable ones. For your bibliographic files, you will only want to do it once—trust us on this. This means that you must convert your files using a standard that can be read and used by most library automation systems so that your bibliographic database will be transportable when you decide to trade in your existing system for a new one. It means getting the fullest and most complete records available so that your public will have the best access possible to all of the information resources you are making available.

The only way to do this is to make sure that your records are in USMARC format. These records are available from a number of bibliographic utilities and vendors either online or on CD-ROM. Several book jobbers will provide a MARC record for a small charge for books you purchase from them. The important thing to remember at this point is to settle for nothing less than full-length, USMARC, bibliographic records.

MICROLIF

This brings us to the issue of MicroLIF. MicroLIF (Microcomputer Library Interchange Format) is a communications standard just as MARC is. It was developed in 1987 by a committee of book and data vendors as a standard for transferring bibliographic data using floppy disks into microcomputer-based systems running library automation software.

Although the committee wanted MicroLIF to be compatible

with the USMARC format, there were deviations. The '91 USMARC MicroLIF protocol, adopted in 1991, is more closely based on the USMARC standard formats and conforms to the USMARC diskette label specifications.

Libraries should require that systems they purchase support the USMARC communications format. Do not accept MicroLIF formats as alternatives. If your current system utilizes the 1987 MicroLIF protocol for record storage, those records must be converted to USMARC, either by machine processing or through another retrospective conversion. Because the '91 USMARC MicroLIF protocol is more closely aligned with USMARC, records stored in this format may need little re-processing to load in the USMARC format. Libraries must determine the formats their bibliographic records are in and take steps, as necessary, to convert them to USMARC format.

CONCLUSION

This has been a very brief introduction to MARC. For those wishing to delve further into MARC's mysteries, see the list of sources.

Following the MARC standard is like following the Yellow Brick Road. You stray from it at your peril, substantially risking your chances of getting to the Emerald City—that is, to a successful automation project—without expensive, sometimes fatal, encounters with the Wicked Witch of Bibliographic Incompatiblity.

SOURCES

Byrne, Deborah J. *MARC Manual: Understanding and Using MARC Records.* 2d ed. Englewood, CO: Libraries Unlimited, forthcoming.

All three types of MARC records—bibliographic, authority, and holdings—are explained, along with specifications for MARC database processing, MARC products, and online systems. The second edition includes a new chapter on MARC format integration and updates all information, including that on MARC authority records and holdings records.

Cataloger's Desktop. Washington, DC: Cataloging Distribution Service, Library of Congress, quarterly subscription.

Offers a wide array of LC cataloging publications, including documentation, on one CD-ROM. The following three USMARC documentation products are on the CD-ROM and are also available individually or as a separate package:

USMARC Format for Authority Data, Including Guidelines for Content Designation. Authority control for both name headings and subjects.

USMARC Format for Bibliographic Data, Including Guidelines for Content Designation. Data elements for bibliographic formats (books, AV manuscripts, maps, music, serials, computer files).

USMARC Format for Holdings Data, Including Guidelines for Content Designation. Format specifications for communicating holdings and location data.

Furrie, Betty. *Understanding MARC.* 4th ed. Washington, DC: Cataloging Distribution Service, 1994.

"This booklet will explain—in the simplest terms possible—what a MARC record is, and it will provide the basic information needed to understand and evaluate a MARC record."

Piepenburg, Scott. *MARC Coding for Automated Systems.* Englewood, CO: Libraries Unlimited, forthcoming.

"Citing real-life examples that might be encountered in a school or small to medium-sized public library, this book familiarizes users with the USMARC bibliographic format. It is structured tag by tag, with the AACR2R for each tag indicated where appropriate. . . . Emphasis is placed on cataloging in an automated environment."

15 STANDARDS

Any library undertaking an automation project should adhere to standards. Standards are sets of specifications that, when conformed to, result in interchangeability and portability of files and networking architectures from one system to another.

Standards allow different systems to interface with one another. There are recognized standards for:

- bibliographic data and formats
- item formats
- transaction formats
- cabling and networking of hardware
- information transfer
- textual data files
- image and multimedia files
- CD-ROM files.

Standards must be proposed to and approved by a national or international standards organization. These organizations include the

- International Standards Organization (ISO)
- National Information Standards Organization (NISO [Z39])*
- American National Standards Institute (ANSI)
- Institute of Electrical and Electronics Engineers (IEEE)
- Telecommunications Industries Association (TIA)
- Internet Engineering Task Force (IETF)
- Electronic Industry Association (EIA).

Some widely adopted documents such as AACR2R and the ALA character set are not standards in the strict sense because they have not been specifically adopted by a recognized standards organization. They have achieved such a high level of acceptance, however, that they are considered de facto standards.

Some standards, particularly those for bibliographic formats, must be implemented by the library prior to the selection and implementation of a system. Others must be required of vendors through an RFP or RFB as part of the procurement process. This

---

* The National Information Standards Organization is a not-for-profit corporation accredited by the American National Standards Institute (ANSI) that develops, maintains, and publishes technical standards used by libraries, information services, and publishers. The standards cited in this book are available in print and CD-ROM formats from NISO (Oxon Hill, MD).

chapter provides an overview of specific standards and why they are important.

BIBLIOGRAPHIC FORMAT AND DATA ELEMENT STANDARDS

Standards for the format and description of bibliographic information in a machine-readable database are important for a number of reasons:

- These standards are well-established and accepted. They are supported by the major bibliographic utilities (e.g., OCLC, RLIN, WLN) and the majority of North American libraries.
- They are critical if libraries are to maintain the portability of their files. Without standards, files cannot easily be transferred from one automated system to another without engaging in a costly, repeat, retrospective conversion project.
- Libraries wishing to participate in resource sharing arrangements with other libraries will find adherence to the standards a condition of participation.

To comply with the standards for formatting and describing bibliographic information, libraries must:

- Use AACR2 Revised, all full MARC formats for bibliographic and authority data, and the International Standard Bibliographic Description (ISBD). The MARC communications formats (see chapter 14) are based on the Information Exchange Format standard (NISO Z39.2/ISO 2709).
- Establish and include in a machine-readable record all critical bibliographic data elements—for example, main entry, title, subtitle, statement of responsibility, edition, and imprint.
- Verify and include data elements unique to the item. These include:
    1. LCCN (Library of Congress Catalog Number)
    2. ISBN (International Standard Book Number, ISO 2108)
    3. ISSN (International Standard Serial Number, ISO 3297)
    4. SICI (Serial Item and Contribution Identifier, Z39.56).

- Require support for:

    1. the American Library Association's Extended ASCII Character Set for Romanized Languages, which is generally the same as NISO Z39.47, ANSEL (Extended Latin Alphabet Coded Character Set for Bibliographic Use)
    2. Unicode (ISO 10646) for non-Romanized languages

- Establish local policy on the treatment of certain bibliographic data elements. For example, should preference be given to the information provided online or to local information (such as local subject headings or notes)? A library might accept without change the record for a straight fiction title, but may wish to make changes in the record for a local history title.
- Establish a hierarchy of acceptance when confronted with multiple full-MARC machine-readable records (such as those of the Library of Congress, National Library of Medicine, or local libraries) for the same bibliographic item.

ITEM FORMATS

Formatting standards and designated fields within the MARC record accommodate the information required to locate and identify an item and enumerate holdings. A new standard—Holdings Statements for Bibliographic Items (NISO Z39.71)—is combining and replacing the previous item standards:

- Serials Holding Statements (NISO Z39.44)
- Holdings Statements for Non-Serial Items (NISO Z39.57)

To properly implement item format standards, libraries must document both current and past entry practices and establish consistent forms of entry for current cataloging. When standardizing item information locally, libraries must:

- Decide on the treatment of and include all critical data elements that provide inventory information on each physical item, including holding library, holding branch, internal location, prefix (Ref, J, etc.), classification number, cutter number, volume data, and serial patterns, enumeration, and chronology.

- Include a unique item identifier (i.e., a bar code number).
- Normalize or standardize inconsistent collection codes and other local designators. (See pages 97–101 for tips on preparing your shelflist for conversion.)

TRANSACTION FORMATS

Two important new standards—Patron Record Data Elements (NISO Z39.69) and Format for Circulation Transactions (NISO Z39.70)—give information in borrower and circulation files the same consistency and portability as data in bibliographic and item files.

The patron data standard will allow the exchange of borrower information for purposes of reciprocal borrowing between and among automated systems. Similarly, circulation information, borrower accounts, hold requests, and scheduling/booking data will be transferable among different systems in compliance with the format for circulation transactions.

CABLING AND NETWORKING OF HARDWARE

Automated library systems now frequently run on networks— local area networks (LANs) and wide area networks (WANs) or metropolitan area networks (MANs)—comprised of personal computers used as servers and workstations. As a result, libraries must be more aware of cabling, network, and telecommunications standards when implementing networks within the library so that existing networks will be compatible with the integrated library systems now on the market.

Some of the major standards are:

- Commercial Building Telecommunications Cabling Standard (EIA/TIA-568A)
- Telecommunications & Information Exchange Between Systems—LANs and MANs (IEEE 802.6)
- Telecommunications & Information Exchange Between Systems (CSMA/CD) (Ethernet) (IEEE 802.3/ISO 8802.3)

- Telecommunications & Information Exchange Between Systems (100VG-AnyLan) (IEEE 802.12)
- Frame Relay (ANSI T1-617-618)
- Asynchronous Transfer Mode (ITU ATM)
- Interface Between Data Terminal Equipment and Data Communication Equipment (EIA RS-232-C-69)
- Small Computer System Interface (SCSI) (ANSI ASC x3.268).

INFORMATION TRANSFER

The ability of automated library systems to interface and interact electronically with one another and with other external information resources is now one of the highest priorities of libraries planning for automation. Successful implementation of these linkages requires adherence to standards and protocols that allow disparate systems to "talk" electronically with each other. These include:

- American Standard Code For Information Exchange (ASCII) (ANSI X3.4)
- Interlibrary Loan Data Elements (NISO Z39.63)
- Open Systems Interconnection (OSI) Reference Model (ISO 7498)
- Transmission Control Protocol/Internet Protocol (ANSI TCP/IP)
- Portable Operating System Interface (POSIX) (IEEE 1003.1/ISO 9945)
- Standards for Programming Languages (ANSI ASC X3)
- Electronic Based Messaging (X.400) (IEEE 1224).
- Information Retrieval Application Service Definition and Protocol Specification for Open System (NISO Z39.50/ISO 23950)

This last standard, popularly known as Z39.50, allows searches initiated in one system to be transmitted to and executed in another system and responses returned to the original system. This standard opens the doors to the world of information by allowing users to tap the resources of collections and databases located outside the four walls of their local library, using the search syntax of their local system.

TEXTUAL, IMAGE, MULTIMEDIA, AND CD-ROM FILE STANDARDS

Automated systems in libraries have traditionally provided circulation control and electronic card catalogs. As we stated at the beginning of the book, all this is changing with the digitization not just of textual resources but also of pictures, sound, and full-motion video. Libraries now expect their automated systems not just to point to information but also to be the gateways through which the information itself flows. This new focus requires a whole new set of standards, many of which are still in development, which leaves de facto standards to be used in the interim.

These standards include formats for transmission of graphic and full-motion images, mark-up languages for the creation of electronic documents, and information exchange formats for CD-ROM hardware and software. They are:

- Graphics Interchange Format (GIF)
- Tagged Image File Format (TIFF)
- Portable Document Format (PDF)
- Digital Compression and Coding of Continuous-Tone Still Images (JPEG—Joint Photographic Experts Group) (ISO/IEC 10918.1)
- Motion Picture Experts Group (MPEG)
- Standard Generalized Markup Language (SGML) (ISO 8879)
- Electronic Manuscript Preparation and Markup (ISO 12083)
- HyperText Markup Language (HTML)
- Common Gateway Interface (CGI)
- Volume & File Structure of CD-ROM for Information Exchange (ISO 9660).

These standards, both official and de facto, are important because any library wishing to provide a gateway to and a presence on the World Wide Web must ensure that its automated system conforms to and supports these protocols. Similarly, transparent access to CD-ROM applications, both multimedia and bibliographic, requires compliance with the CD-ROM information exchange standard.

SOURCES

Boss, Richard W. "Standards for Automated Library Systems and Other Information Technologies." *Library Technology Reports* 32:4 (July–August 1996), 461–564.

"[A] practical handbook for persons writing standards specifications as part of a procurement document." Chapter 1 defines "standards," reviews their role, and describes the major standards organizations. Chapters 2 through 7 discuss specific standards, by type: format (e.g., MARC), cabling and networks (telecommunications), interfaces (for linking systems within and between libraries and other organizations, e.g., Z39.50), business communication (for communicating with book and serial vendors and jobbers, e.g., EDI, EDIFACT), and image (e.g., GIF, TIFF), full-text (e.g., HTML), and CD-ROM standards. There is language for an RFP, a glossary, and a bibliography.

Crawford, Walt. *Technical Standards: An Introduction for Librarians.* 2d ed. Boston: G.K. Hall, 1991. *Out of print.*

Examines the overall field, providing definitions and reviewing problems as well as how changes are implemented. Part 2 deals with NISO—the National Information Standards Organization—and explains how standards are developed.

"Perspectives on . . . Information Technology Standards." *Journal of the American Society for Information Science* 43:8 (September 1992), 521–578.

This entire issue of *JASIS* is devoted to "the current work and thinking on information technology standardization—from Z39.50 to X.25, from acid-free paper standards to the growth of SGML and Z39.59." The articles offer "perspectives from both academics and practitioners, with a multidisciplinary focus."

CONCLUSION: PLANNING FOR THE FUTURE

Planning has gained such widespread acceptance in the profession that experience and familiarity with planning can truly be considered an essential skill for every librarian. Planning process methodologies are now the norm in corporations, education, and government, and librarians must master planning concepts and methodologies if they are to function effectively within their parent organizations and funding environments.

Plans must be regularly revisited and updated as the environment and needs change. In general, a library should review its plans on an annual basis and conduct a major reexamination of its plans every five years. Luckily, this is facilitated because virtually every library prepares some form of report for its public, funding authority, or parent organization on an annual basis. By incorporating a planning review into this process, annual reports can move from a statement of past accomplishments to an opportunity to make others aware of your goals and objectives and to lay the groundwork for your funding request.

An annual review of library automation should be part of this review process because, like your five-year plan, automated systems change with time.

THE LIFE CYCLE OF AUTOMATED SYSTEMS

THE BAD NEWS: OBSOLESCENCE

As we have come to understand, computer technology and software applications change and evolve at an incredibly rapid pace. At current rates of development, you can expect that by the time you install your carefully planned system, capabilities will be available that were only in planning stages while you were evaluating vendor proposals. In computing technology, there is a cynical maxim: "If it works, it must be obsolete."

How long can you expect to be happy with your new system before changes in computer technology and functionality will render it "obsolete"? Normally, a life cycle of five years is considered acceptable for a computer system before some significant upgrade (installation of additional hardware and/or software providing for increased capability or capacity) or replacement becomes necessary. You must also consider the rapid changes occurring in the telecommunications field and the formulation and reformulation of standards designed to strengthen system performance and interconnectivity.

Accordingly, libraries must not give their parent organizations and/or funding authorities the impression that planning for and implementing automation is a "one-shot" proposition. From the first, policymakers must be educated to realize that advances in computer and information technology represent a fundamental change in the way libraries do business and require an ongoing commitment to keep pace with the changing and evolving world of information technology.

Why do systems need to be upgraded? For one or more of the following reasons:

- The library is ready to add new functionality.
- The library has exceeded the capacity of the original system.
- Current software must be upgraded because newer versions have been issued and current versions are no longer supported by the vendor.
- Original hardware and telecommunications equipment must be replaced.
- The vendor no longer supports the system or has ceased operation.

Happily, the vast majority of upgrades are undertaken because the library is ready for new functionality or capacity. Just keep in mind that no system lasts forever—nor will you want it to.

THE GOOD NEWS: IMPROVED SERVICE

The positive side of the picture is that, due to rapid advances in technology, we can expect tremendous increases in our ability to access, store, and process information within the library. What began with automating backroom processes has evolved to the ubiquity of powerful workstations on people's desktops. Future developments that are virtually assured include:

- There will be an exponential growth in the number of individuals and organizations using electronic technology, such as homepages and "freenets" to produce and/or make available vast amounts of information that would never have existed or been accessible in a print environment.

- Libraries will remain print oriented overall, but reference services will become essentially electronically based rather than book based.
- There will exist far greater interactivity between and among integrated systems, improving access to information and changing individual "local systems" into "nodes" within large, client/server-based, distributed networks.
- Traditional library functions will continue to appear less like discrete modules and more like processes along a continuum of functionality within automated systems.
- Library users and staff will gain greater control over the access tools in libraries, shaping previously static devices such as catalogs (card or computer) into individually customizable front-ends to their library's (and other libraries') information resources.
- Librarians themselves will play a greater role in the creation, packaging, and distribution of information, adding greater value to the material they make available to their users.
- Library users will have selective dissemination of information-type services available to them through libraries of all types, with the library using automation to create customized reading files on an ongoing basis from a variety of electronic sources and tailored to the user's individual interests and needs.

Remember: With every step you take, you are one step closer to bringing these exciting possibilities to your users—and you are gaining valuable experience and knowledge that will promote more effective planning and decision making in the future.

THE BENEFITS OF GOOD PLANNING

In summary, the results of good planning are:

- confidence that you have selected the *best possible system* available, given technological and financial constraints
- confidence that you have addressed the *priority needs* of your library
- confidence that you have established a firm basis of understanding and a methodology (the planning process) for *future planning*

- confidence on the part of your parent organization or funding authority that automation activities are being implemented as part of a clearly articulated, overall plan for the *development of library services*
- confidence that you have the ability to respond quickly and effectively to *unexpected opportunities and challenges* in automation and in other areas, with a clear understanding of how these unexpected developments and technological changes may be used to support the library's long-range goals.

APPENDIX: WORKING WITH CONSULTANTS

Many libraries engaged in automation planning will at one time or another consider securing the services of a consultant. An automation consultant will function in one or more of the following capacities:

- *Objective Outsider/Authority:* The consultant is employed as an expert who will examine the library and its operations and recommend actions. If the consultant is a recognized authority, his or her recommendations may be more easily accepted by a funding agency or parent organization.
- *Technical Advisor:* The consultant works with library planners to provide specific information on the technical aspects of automation, system capabilities, or evaluation of vendor proposals, thereby supporting the decision-making process rather than making decisions.
- *Trainer/Educator:* The consultant educates planners and parent organization members through a series of structured training activities, providing planners with the technical knowledge they need to make decisions.
- *Process Leader:* The consultant provides a structure for one or more parts of the planning process, supporting group decision-making processes. Examples might include working with staff to develop and prioritize needs, develop specifications, or evaluate proposals.
- *Task Manager:* The consultant is hired to complete a specific task, such as a shelflist analysis, writing a request-for-proposal, or a bar code labeling project. The consultant's involvement ends when the task is completed.

It is often useful to retain a consultant early in the planning process to give staff and planners an overview of automation concepts and options and the automation planning process. In many instances, consulting of this type is available from state agencies or consortia at little or no cost. Alternatively, staff may be able to attend continuing education programs and seminars offered off-site through professional agencies, state agencies, consortia, or consultants. Either way, remember to have as many staff as possible participate. Education is a modest expense that will yield real returns throughout the planning process.

If you intend to utilize a consultant in the system selection process, it is best if you also involve the consultant in the development of system specifications and identification of priorities (see below). That way, the consultant will have a firm understanding of the library's needs when the selection is made.

FINDING A CONSULTANT

If your library has decided to use a consultant, the first thing you will need to do is develop a written description of what the consultant will do. Keeping in mind the roles outlined earlier, this description should include:

- steps of the planning process in which the consultant will be involved
- the consultant's responsibilities at each step
- meetings the consultant will attend and with whom the consultant will meet (on-site consulting days)
- written and/or oral reports the consultant will present and to whom they will be presented
- a desired time line for the above activities
- a request for a cost proposal, a statement of qualifications, and a list of previous clients.

This document should then be distributed to appropriate consultants. Names of potential consultants may be garnered from professional associations and from state and cooperative library agencies and directories. Your library may also advertise its interest in receiving proposals in one or more appropriate professional publications with wide distribution.

SELECTING A CONSULTANT

Normally, the result of your efforts will be the receipt of one or more proposals from consultants. In selecting the consultant, the following criteria should be kept in mind:

1. the degree to which the consultant's proposal matches your requirements

2. the consultant's experience in assisting similar libraries with similar projects
3. positive evaluations from previous clients
4. proposed costs.

To standardize the evaluation process, those involved in selecting the consultant should give each proposal a rating based on each of the criteria. This will help make the selection process more objective—and it provides good practice for the system selection process. Once the field has been narrowed down, an in-person meeting with each candidate (if possible) will assist your planning committee in assessing such factors as style and interpersonal skills.

THE CONSULTANT AGREEMENT

Once you have selected your consultant, you must confirm in writing all of the specifics included in your proposal and in the response. At a minimum, a letter should specify the number of on-site consulting days, any reports to be provided, and the total cost of services to be provided. It also can be useful to agree on a per diem rate for additional work that the library may wish the consultant to provide later on in the planning process. With clear requirements and a specific written agreement, both you and your consultant should have the same expectations.

ETHICAL ISSUES IN AUTOMATION CONSULTING

As the library-consultant relationship develops, all parties should remain aware of important standards of behavior that will enhance the outcome of the consultation process. A few of these, with particular relevance to automation consulting, may be outlined as follows:

1. The client library has a responsibility to maintain a proper and correct relationship with prospective consultants and with the consultant it selects. This includes:

- preparing an accurate and complete RFP—one that fully presents the library's automation-related purposes in retaining a consultant's services.
- genuinely seeking its consultant's expertise and recommendations in an open decision-making process, i.e., the library has not already made its decisions.
- moving ahead with decisions, system requirements, and the like that represent the work that has been done and not making alterations without informing the consultant.
- remembering that materials developed by the library's consultant are proprietary.

2. The consultant has a responsibility to maintain his or her objectivity and lack of bias throughout the process. This means:

- honestly representing his or her skills, background, and references in any response to an RFP for consulting services.
- cooperating with the client library but not acquiescing when, in his or her best professional judgment, the library's expectations are counterproductive to the process.
- working to develop a solution that meets the library's needs as opposed to offering a favorite solution out of context.
- being open about any relationships he or she may have with a prospective automation vendor and not concealing any potential conflicts of interest.

3. Both the client library and the consultant have a responsibility to:

- Insure an open, honest process in securing vendor services for automation. Most especially, this means not "wiring a bid," i.e., preparing an inherently biased RFP or similar document that wastes the time and efforts of vendors responding in good faith but who, in reality, have been excluded before the fact.
- Maintain confidentiality on all matters pertaining to the consultation, particularly when a competitive process for providing services or systems is involved.
- Maintain a professional relationship at all times, including the avoidance of "finger-pointing" if problems or disagreements develop.

MAKING THE MOST OF YOUR CONSULTANT

It is not always possible or desirable to use a consultant. When used effectively, however, consultants can save time, may save money, and may help you feel confident that you are making the best possible decision given the available options.

Libraries often bring unrealistic expectations to consulting situations. More realistic expectations and an understanding of consultant roles will help prevent disappointment and ensure the most effective results when you do use a consultant. *Consultants cannot and should not take the place of active administrative and staff involvement in the automation planning process.*

If you use a consultant, keep in mind that the consultant's job is not to make the decision for you, but to assist you in obtaining background and technical information and establishing a structure within which you can make your own decisions. After all, you and your staff understand your library and its patrons better than any consultant can hope to. And in the long run, the most successful automation planning is based on decisions made by the library's staff. The long process of education, prioritization, identification of alternatives, evaluation, and selection will be the best guarantee of satisfaction with the results.

SOURCES

Garten, Edward D., ed. *Using Consultants in Libraries and Information Centers: A Management Handbook.* Westport, CT: Greenwood, 1992.

Essays explore establishing the reasons for using a consultant, processes for insuring a successful consulting relationship, using a consultant for various purposes, ethical issues and dilemmas, and alternative methods for securing consulting expertise. Edwin M. Cortez and Susan Baerg Epstein, respectively, write about the role of consultants in the development of RFPs and in contract negotiations. M.E.L. Jacob discusses using consultants in the strategic planning process. Nancy Courtney and Anita Johnson offer a useful concluding bibliographic essay on "resources and readings" published between 1970 and 1991.

Holtz, Herman. *Choosing and Using a Consultant: A Manager's Guide to Consulting Services.* New York: Wiley, 1989.

Covers how to know when you need a consultant (assessing your need), how to find consultants, soliciting and evaluating bids, negotiations, and cost guidelines. Deals with common problems, how to maintain good relations, and the final evaluation of your consultant's work.

Matthews, Joseph R. "The Effective Use of Consultants in Libraries." *Library Technology Reports* 30:6 (November/December 1994), 745–814. Edited by Howard S. White. American Library Association.

This "Report" within *LTR* reviews all aspects of finding, hiring and working with a consultant. There is a section on codes of practice, guidelines, and standards (pp. 767–778).

Shenson, Howard L. *How to Select and Manage Consultants: A Guide to Getting What You Pay For.* Lexington, MA: D.C. Heath, 1990.

Discusses consultant roles, finding and evaluating consultants, fees, proposals, and contracts. Sample consultant proposals and letters of agreement are included, as is a critical, annotated bibliography.

INDEX

COLOPHON

John M. Cohn and Ann L. Kelsey are Director and Associate Director respectively of the Sherman H. Masten Learning Resource Center at the County College of Morris in Randolph, New Jersey, and partners in DocuMentors, an independent consulting firm.

Keith Michael Fiels is Director of the Massachusetts Board of Library Commissioners in Boston.